LIFE
Lessons
WITH MAX LUCADO

BOOK OF
MATTHEW

THE CARPENTER KING

MAX LUCADO

Prepared by
THE LIVINGSTONE CORPORATION

Published by
THOMAS NELSON™
Since 1798

www.thomasnelson.com

Life Lessons with Max Lucado—Book of Matthew

Copyright © by Thomas Nelson, 2007

Published in Nashville, Tennessee. Thomas Nelson is a trademark of Thomas Nelson, Inc.

Thomas Nelson, Inc. titles may be purchased in bulk for educational, business, fundraising, or sales promotional use. For information, please email SpecialMarkets@ThomasNelson.com.

Scripture passages taken from:
The Holy Bible, New Century Version (NCV). Copyright ©1987, 1988, 1991 by Word Publishing. All rights reserved.
The Holy Bible, New King James Version (NKJV). Copyright © 1979, 1980, 1982 by Thomas Nelson. All rights reserved.
The HOLY BIBLE, NEW INTERNATIONAL VERSION® (NIV). Copyright © 1973, 1978, 1984 by International Bible Society. Used by permission of Zondervan Publishing House. All rights reserved. The "NIV" and "New International Version" trademarks are registered in the United States Patent and Trademark Office by International Bible Society. Use of either trademark requires the permission of International Bible Society.
The *Holy Bible,* New Living Translation (NLT). Copyright © 1996, 2004. Used by permission of Tyndale House Publishers, Inc., Wheaton, Illinois 60189. All rights reserved.

Material for the "Inspiration" sections taken from the following books:
And the Angels Were Silent. Copyright © 1992, 2004 by Max Lucado. W Publishing Group, a Division of Thomas Nelson, Inc., Nashville, Tennessee.
The Applause of Heaven. Copyright © 1990, 1996, 1999 by Max Lucado. W Publishing Group, a Division of Thomas Nelson, Inc., Nashville, Tennessee.
Come Thirsty. Copyright © 2004 by Max Lucado. W Publishing Group, a Division of Thomas Nelson, Inc., Nashville, Tennessee.
Cure for the Common Life. Copyright © 2005 by Max Lucado. W Publishing Group, a Division of Thomas Nelson, Inc., Nashville, Tennessee.
A Gentle Thunder, Copyright © 1995 by Max Lucado. W Publishing Group, a Division of Thomas Nelson, Inc., Nashville, Tennessee.
In the Eye of the Storm. Copyright © 1991 by Max Lucado. W Publishing Group, a Division of Thomas Nelson, Inc., Nashville, Tennessee.
Just Like Jesus. Copyright © 1998 by Max Lucado. W Publishing Group, a Division of Thomas Nelson, Inc., Nashville, Tennessee.
Next Door Savior. Copyright © 2003 by Max Lucado. W Publishing Group, a Division of Thomas Nelson, Inc., Nashville, Tennessee.
Traveling Light. Copyright © 2001 by Max Lucado. W Publishing Group, a Division of Thomas Nelson, Inc., Nashville, Tennessee.
When Christ Comes Copyright © 1999 by Max Lucado. W Publishing Group, a Division of Thomas Nelson, Inc., Nashville, Tennessee.

Produced with the assistance of the Livingstone Corporation. Project staff include Jake Barton, Joel Bartlett, Andy Culbertson, Mary Horner Collins, Will Reaves, and Rachel Hawkins.
Editor: Len Woods
Cover Art and Interior Design by Kirk Luttrell of the Livingstone Corporation
Interior Composition by Rachel Hawkins of the Livingstone Corporation

ISBN-10: 1-4185-0969-8
ISBN-13: 978-1-4185-0969-9

Printed in the United States of America.
07 08 QG 9 8 7 6 5 4 3 2 1

LIFE Lessons

WITH MAX LUCADO

CONTENTS

HOW TO STUDY THE BIBLE

This is a peculiar book you are holding. Words crafted in another language. Deeds done in a distant era. Events recorded in a far-off land. Counsel offered to a foreign people. This is a peculiar book.

It's surprising that anyone reads it. It's too old. Some of its writings date back five thousand years. It's too bizarre. The book speaks of incredible floods, fires, earthquakes, and people with supernatural abilities. It's too radical. The Bible calls for undying devotion to a carpenter who called himself God's Son.

Logic says this book shouldn't survive. Too old, too bizarre, too radical.

The Bible has been banned, burned, scoffed, and ridiculed. Scholars have mocked it as foolish. Kings have branded it as illegal. A thousand times over, the grave has been dug and the dirge has begun, but somehow the Bible never stays in the grave. Not only has it survived; it has thrived. It is the single most popular book in all of history. It has been the best-selling book in the world for years!

There is no way on earth to explain it. Which perhaps is the only explanation. The answer? The Bible's durability is not found on earth; it is found in heaven. For the millions who have tested its claims and claimed its promises, there is but one answer: the Bible is God's book and God's voice.

As you read it, you would be wise to give some thought to two questions. What is the purpose of the Bible? and How do I study the Bible? Time spent reflecting on these two issues will greatly enhance your Bible study.

What is the purpose of the Bible?

Let the Bible itself answer that question.

Since you were a child you have known the Holy Scriptures which are able to make you wise. And that wisdom leads to salvation through faith in Christ Jesus. (2 Tim. 3:15 NCV)

The purpose of the Bible? Salvation. God's highest passion is to get his children home. His book, the Bible, describes his plan of salvation. The purpose of the Bible is to proclaim God's plan and passion to save his children.

That is the reason this book has endured through the centuries. It dares to tackle the toughest questions about life: Where do I go after I die? Is there a God? What do I do with my fears? The Bible offers answers to these crucial questions. It is the treasure map that leads us to God's highest treasure, eternal life.

QG 06-22-12

But how do we use the Bible? Countless copies of Scripture sit unread on bookshelves and nightstands simply because people don't know how to read it. What can we do to make the Bible real in our lives?

The clearest answer is found in the words of Jesus. He promised:

Ask, and God will give to you. Search, and you will find. Knock, and the door will open for you. (Matt. 7:7 NCV)

The first step in understanding the Bible is asking God to help us. We should read prayerfully. If anyone understands God's Word, it is because of God and not the reader.

But the Helper will teach you everything and will cause you to remember all that I told you. The Helper is the Holy Spirit whom the Father will send in my name. (John 14:26 NCV)

Before reading the Bible, pray. Invite God to speak to you. Don't go to Scripture looking for your idea; go searching for his.

Not only should we read the Bible prayerfully; we should read it carefully. *Search and you will find* is the pledge. The Bible is not a newspaper to be skimmed but rather a mine to be quarried.

Search for it like silver, and hunt for it like hidden treasure. Then you will understand respect for the LORD, and you will find that you know God. (Prov. 2:4–5 NCV)

Any worthy find requires effort. The Bible is no exception. To understand the Bible you don't have to be brilliant, but you must be willing to roll up your sleeves and search.

Be a worker who is not ashamed and who uses the true teaching in the right way. (2 Tim. 2:15 NCV)

Here's a practical point. Study the Bible a bit at a time. Hunger is not satisfied by eating twenty-one meals in one sitting once a week. The body needs a steady diet to remain strong. So does the soul. When God sent food to his people in the wilderness, he didn't provide loaves already made. Instead, he sent them manna in the shape of *"thin flakes like frost . . . on the desert ground"* (Ex. 16:14 NCV).

God gave manna in limited portions. God sends spiritual food the same way. He opens the heavens with just enough nutrients for today's hunger. He provides *"a command here, a command there. A rule here, a rule there. A little lesson here, a little lesson there"* (Isa. 28:10 NCV).

Don't be discouraged if your reading reaps a small harvest. Some days a lesser portion is all that is needed. What is important is to search every day for that day's message. A steady diet of God's Word over a lifetime builds a healthy soul and mind.

A little girl returned from her first day at school. Her mom asked, "Did you learn anything?"

"Apparently not enough," the girl responded, "I have to go back tomorrow and the next day and the next . . ."

Such is the case with learning. And such is the case with Bible study. Understanding comes little by little over a lifetime.

There is a third step in understanding the Bible. After the asking and seeking comes the knocking. After you ask and search, then knock.

Knock, and the door will open for you. (Matt. 7:7 NCV)

To knock is to stand at God's door. To make yourself available. To climb the steps, cross the porch, stand at the doorway, and volunteer. Knocking goes beyond the realm of thinking and into the realm of acting.

To knock is to ask, What can I do? How can I obey? Where can I go?

It's one thing to know what to do. It's another to do it. But for those who do it, those who choose to obey, a special reward awaits them.

The truly happy are those who carefully study God's perfect law that makes people free, and they continue to study it. They do not forget what they heard, but they obey what God's teaching says. Those who do this will be made happy. (James 1:25 NCV)

What a promise. Happiness comes to those who do what they read! It's the same with medicine. If you only read the label but ignore the pills, it won't help. It's the same with food. If you only read the recipe but never cook, you won't be fed. And it's the same with the Bible. If you only read the words but never obey, you'll never know the joy God has promised.

Ask. Search. Knock. Simple, isn't it? Why don't you give it a try? If you do, you'll see why you are holding the most remarkable book in history.

INTRODUCTION TO THE BOOK OF MATTHEW

You gotta wonder what Jesus saw in Matthew.

He was a tax collector. The profession hasn't been too popular in any era, but especially not in the days of Christ. Tax collectors were the quislings of Palestine. They took from their own people and gave to Rome. As long as they met their quota, they could tax whatever they wanted and as much as they wanted.

Not only was Matthew a tax collector; he was a public tax collector. Some collectors did their business underground. They hired runners to do their dirty work. Matthew did his own. He was the leech at the bottom of the pit. He pulled his stretch limo right into the greasiest parts of town and set up his table and held out his hand.

That's where he was when Jesus called him.

You gotta wonder what Jesus saw in Matthew. At the same time, you gotta wonder what Matthew saw in Jesus. I mean, look at him. Dirt under his nails. Calloused hands. Holes in his sandals. No headquarters. No office. No committee. No clout with the local church.

The clergy won't give him the time of day. His followers look more like dockhands or pool sharks than seminarians.

This guy claims to be the Messiah?

Quite a pair, these two. But Matthew accepted Christ's invitation and never turned back. He spent the rest of his life convincing folks that this carpenter was the King. Jesus gave the call and never took it back. The relationship Jesus had with Matthew can serve to convince us that if Jesus had a place for Matthew, he just might have a place for us.

LESSON ONE

GOD WITH SKIN ON

MAX
LUCADO

REFLECTION

Each December Christians look back on the mind-boggling events of that first Christmas—angel armies appearing to awestruck shepherds, the star of Bethlehem guiding the wise men, and, of course, the baby in the manger. What do you do each holiday season to remember and savor the stunning claim of the gospel—that God took on flesh and made his dwelling among us?

SITUATION

Writing to his fellow Jews, Matthew begins his Gospel by demonstrating that Jesus descended (humanly speaking) from both Abraham and King David. He then discusses some of the circumstances surrounding Christ's virgin birth and stormy infancy.

OBSERVATION

Read Matthew 1:18–2:12 from the NCV or the NKJV.

NCV

18This is how the birth of Jesus Christ came about. His mother Mary was engaged to marry Joseph, but before they married, she learned she was pregnant by the power of the Holy Spirit. 19Because Mary's husband, Joseph, was a good man, he did not want to disgrace her in public, so he planned to divorce her secretly.

20While Joseph thought about these things, an angel of the Lord came to him in a dream. The angel said, "Joseph, descendant of David, don't be afraid to take Mary as your wife, because the baby in her is from the Holy Spirit. 21She will give birth to a son, and you will name him Jesus, because he will save his people from their sins."

22All this happened to bring about what the Lord had said through the prophet: 23"The virgin will be pregnant. She will have a son, and they will name him Immanuel," which means "God is with us."

24When Joseph woke up, he did what the Lord's angel had told him to do. Joseph took Mary as his wife, 25but he did not have sexual relations with her until she gave birth to the son. And Joseph named him Jesus.

2:1Jesus was born in the town of Bethlehem in Judea during the time when Herod was king. When Jesus was born, some wise men from the east came to Jerusalem. 2They asked, "Where is the baby who was born to be the king of the Jews? We saw his star in the east and have come to worship him."

3When King Herod heard this, he was troubled, as well as all the people in Jerusalem. 4Herod called a meeting of all the leading priests and teachers of the law and asked them where the Christ would be born. 5They answered, "In the town of Bethlehem in Judea. The prophet wrote about this in the Scriptures:

6'But you, Bethlehem, in the land of Judah,

are important among the tribes of Judah.

A ruler will come from you

who will be like a shepherd for my people Israel.'"

7Then Herod had a secret meeting with the wise men and learned from them the exact time they first saw the star. 8He sent the wise men to Bethlehem, saying, "Look carefully for the child. When you find him, come tell me so I can worship him too."

9After the wise men heard the king, they left. The star that they had seen in the east went before them until it stopped above the place where the child was. 10When the wise men saw the star, they were filled with joy. 11They came to the house where the child was and saw him with his mother, Mary, and they bowed down and worshiped him. They opened their gifts and gave him treasures of gold, frankincense, and myrrh. 12But God warned the wise men in a dream not to go back to Herod, so they returned to their own country by a different way.

NKJV

1:18Now the birth of Jesus Christ was as follows: After His mother Mary was betrothed to Joseph, before they came together, she was found with child of the Holy Spirit. 19Then Joseph her husband, being a just man, and not wanting to make her a public example, was minded to put her away secretly. 20But while he thought about these things, behold, an angel of the Lord appeared to him in a dream, saying, "Joseph, son of David, do not be afraid to take to you Mary your wife, for that which is conceived in her is of the Holy Spirit. 21And she will bring forth a Son, and you shall call His name JESUS, for He will save His people from their sins."

22So all this was done that it might be fulfilled which was spoken by the Lord through the prophet, saying: 23"Behold, the virgin shall be with child, and bear a Son, and they shall call His name Immanuel," which is translated, "God with us."

24Then Joseph, being aroused from sleep, did as the angel of the Lord commanded him and took to him his wife, 25and did not know her till she had brought forth her firstborn Son. And he called His name JESUS.

2:1Now after Jesus was born in Bethlehem of Judea in the days of Herod the king, behold, wise men from the East came to Jerusalem, 2saying, "Where is He who has been born King of the Jews? For we have seen His star in the East and have come to worship Him."

³When Herod the king heard this, he was troubled, and all Jerusalem with him. ⁴And when he had gathered all the chief priests and scribes of the people together, he inquired of them where the Christ was to be born.

⁵So they said to him, "In Bethlehem of Judea, for thus it is written by the prophet:

⁶'But you, Bethlehem, in the land of Judah,

Are not the least among the rulers of Judah;

For out of you shall come a Ruler

Who will shepherd My people Israel.'"

⁷Then Herod, when he had secretly called the wise men, determined from them what time the star appeared. ⁸And he sent them to Bethlehem and said, "Go and search carefully for the young Child, and when you have found Him, bring back word to me, that I may come and worship Him also."

⁹When they heard the king, they departed; and behold, the star which they had seen in the East went before them, till it came and stood over where the young Child was. ¹⁰When they saw the star, they rejoiced with exceedingly great joy. ¹¹And when they had come into the house, they saw the young Child with Mary His mother, and fell down and worshiped Him. And when they had opened their treasures, they presented gifts to Him: gold, frankincense, and myrrh.

¹²Then, being divinely warned in a dream that they should not return to Herod, they departed for their own country another way.

EXPLORATION

1. Why would Christ's ancestry have mattered to the first Jewish readers of Matthew's Gospel?

2. It is often said, "Things are not what they seem to be." How does this statement apply to Mary's pregnancy and the coming of Christ into the world?

3. What can we learn about Joseph's character from Matthew 1 and 2?

4. What was Herod's response to the news that Christ, "the king of the Jews," had come?

5. Why do you think wise men from the East traveled so far and so long to find Christ, while Israel's religious scholars and leaders didn't look for him at all?

INSPIRATION

The babe of Bethlehem. Immanuel. Remember the promise of the angel? *"'Behold, the virgin shall be with child, and bear a Son, and they shall call His name Immanuel,' which is translated, 'God with us'"* (Matt. 1:23 NKJV).

Immanuel. The name appears in the same Hebrew form as it did two thousand years ago. "Immanu" means "with us." "El" refers to Elohim, or God. Not an "above us God" or a "somewhere in the neighborhood God." He came as the "with us God," God with us.

Not "God with the rich" or "God with the religious." But God with *us*. All of us. Russians, Germans, Buddhists, Mormons, truck drivers and taxi drivers, librarians. God with *us*.

God *with* us. Don't we love the word "with"? "Will you go *with* me?" we ask. "To the store, to the hospital, through my life?" God says he will. "I am *with* you always," Jesus said before he ascended to heaven, "to the very end of the age" (Matt. 28:20 NIV). Search for restrictions on the promise; you'll find none. You won't find "I'll be with you if you behave . . . when you believe. I'll be with you on Sundays in worship . . . at mass." No, none of that. There's no withholding tax on God's "with" promise. He is *with* us.

God is with us.

Prophets weren't enough. Apostles wouldn't do. Angels won't suffice. God sent more than miracles and messages. He sent himself; he sent his Son. "The Word became flesh and dwelt among us" (John 1:14 NKJV). (From *Cure for the Common Life* by Max Lucado)

REACTION

6. When was the last time you were really struck by the biblical claim that for three decades, the Creator actually moved into the midst of his creation in the person of Jesus Christ?

7. What do you think has helped or hindered your unchurched neighbors and coworkers in truly grasping that Jesus is God incarnate?

8. When has God seemed the most real, the most tangible, the most *near* to you?

9. What lessons can you learn from Joseph about submitting to the big purposes of God?

10. How do the wise men on the one hand and King Herod on the other represent the two divergent responses most people have to Christ?

11. The wise men gave so much to Christ—their attention, time, energy, effort, affection, worship, wealth, etc. They risked their lives and perhaps also their careers, credibility, and reputations. Take a moment to assess your life and your devotion to Christ. Right now what specifically are you giving him?

LIFE LESSONS

If we ever begin to doubt God's love for us, we need look no further than the child of Bethlehem. That's no mere infant lying there in the feeding trough—he's Deity in diapers. The universe watched with wonder as heaven's (and earth's) King learned to walk. Jesus would grow up in a Jewish home. For thirty-three years he would feel everything you and I have ever felt. Weakness. Weariness. Fear of failure. Temptation. Fully human, we can safely assume Christ got colds and that he stumped his toes. His feelings got hurt. His feet got tired. And his head ached.

To think of Jesus in such a light is—well, it seems almost irreverent, doesn't it? It's not something we like to do; it's uncomfortable. It is much easier to keep the humanity out of the incarnation. But it's also unbiblical. Christ was God . . . with skin on.

DEVOTION

Father, thank you for sending your Son to be with us and to die for us. Jesus, thank you for being my personal Savior. Spirit of God, open my eyes to the wondrous truth of the gospel. May I daily be amazed by grace. May I walk in your power. May I have courage and joy to share the good news of Immanuel, God with us.

For more Bible passages on the Incarnation, see Isaiah 7:14; Luke 1:26—2:21; and John 1:1—18.

To complete the book of Matthew during this twelve-part study, read Matthew 1:1—2:23.

JOURNALING

How would my life tomorrow be different if I could live continually with an awareness that Christ is with me and in me?

LESSON TWO

OVERCOMING
TEMPTATION

MAX
LUCADO

REFLECTION

Even more certain than death, hunger, and taxes is the reality of temptation. And worse, as someone has quipped, temptations are like stray cats—treat one nicely, and before you can blink, it'll be back with a dozen of its friends! How would you define temptation to a child? Describe the process of being lured into sin.

SITUATION

Matthew, like the other Gospel writers, wastes little time in getting to the beginning of Christ's public ministry. He describes the Lord's baptism and his temptation in the wilderness. Then we watch him choose some disciples as he begins to teach the good news about the kingdom of heaven.

OBSERVATION

Read Matthew 4:1–11 from the NCV or the NKJV.

NCV

¹Then the Spirit led Jesus into the desert to be tempted by the devil. ²Jesus ate nothing for forty days and nights. After this, he was very hungry. ³The devil came to Jesus to tempt him, saying, "If you are the Son of God, tell these rocks to become bread."

⁴Jesus answered, "It is written in the Scriptures, 'A person does not live by eating only bread, but by everything God says.' "

⁵*Then the devil led Jesus to the holy city of Jerusalem and put him on a high place of the Temple.* ⁶*The devil said, "If you are the Son of God, jump down, because it is written in the Scriptures:*

'He has put his angels in charge of you.

They will catch you in their hands

so that you will not hit your foot on a rock.'"

⁷*Jesus answered him, "It also says in the Scriptures, 'Do not test the Lord your God.'"*

⁸*Then the devil led Jesus to the top of a very high mountain and showed him all the kingdoms of the world and all their splendor.* ⁹*The devil said, "If you will bow down and worship me, I will give you all these things."*

¹⁰*Jesus said to the devil, "Go away from me, Satan! It is written in the Scriptures, 'You must worship the Lord your God and serve only him.'"*

¹¹*So the devil left Jesus, and angels came and took care of him.*

NKJV

¹*Then Jesus was led up by the Spirit into the wilderness to be tempted by the devil.* ²*And when He had fasted forty days and forty nights, afterward He was hungry.* ³*Now when the tempter came to Him, he said, "If You are the Son of God, command that these stones become bread."*

⁴*But He answered and said, "It is written, 'Man shall not live by bread alone, but by every word that proceeds from the mouth of God.' "*

⁵*Then the devil took Him up into the holy city, set Him on the pinnacle of the temple,* ⁶*and said to Him, "If You are the Son of God, throw Yourself down. For it is written:*

'He shall give His angels charge over you,' and

'In their hands they shall bear you up,

Lest you dash your foot against a stone.'"

⁷*Jesus said to him, "It is written again, 'You shall not tempt the LORD your God.'"*

⁸*Again, the devil took Him up on an exceedingly high mountain, and showed Him all the kingdoms of the world and their glory.* ⁹*And he said to Him, "All these things I will give You if You will fall down and worship me."*

¹⁰*Then Jesus said to him, "Away with you, Satan! For it is written, 'You shall worship the LORD your God, and Him only you shall serve.'"*

¹¹*Then the devil left Him, and behold, angels came and ministered to Him.*

EXPLORATION

1. Take a few moments to look at the context of the passage you've just read. What was John the Baptist's role in the ministry of Christ?

2. Look carefully at the sequence of events in 3:16—4:2. Does anything seem odd or ironic about it?

3. What would have been so wrong with turning stones into bread? (After all, eating is not a sin.)

4. What do you think Jesus felt in the midst of this time of testing? How does this differ with how he responded?

5. How did the devil misuse Scripture to try to entice Jesus to act independently of the Father?

INSPIRATION

Have you ever thought about the evil things done to Christ? Can you think of times when Jesus could have given up? How about his time of temptation? You and I know what it is like to endure a moment of temptation or an hour of temptation, even a day of temptation. But forty days? That is what Jesus faced. *"The Spirit led Jesus into the desert where the devil tempted Jesus for forty days"* (Luke 4:1–2 NCV).

We imagine the wilderness temptation as three isolated events scattered over a forty-day period. Would that it had been. In reality, Jesus' time of testing was nonstop; "the devil tempted Jesus for forty days." Satan got on Jesus like a shirt and refused to leave. Every step, whispering in his ear. Every turn of the path, sowing doubt. Was Jesus impacted by the devil? Apparently so. Luke doesn't say that Satan *tried* to tempt Jesus. The verse doesn't read, the devil *attempted* to tempt Jesus. No the passage is clear: "the devil *tempted* Jesus." Jesus was *tempted,* he was *tested.* Tempted to change sides? Tempted to go home? Tempted to settle for a kingdom on earth? I don't know, but I know he was tempted. A war raged within. Stress stormed without. And since he was tempted, he could have quit the race. But he didn't. He kept on running.

Temptation didn't stop him, nor did accusations. Can you imagine what it would be like to run in a race and be criticized by the bystanders?

Some years ago I entered a five-K race. Nothing serious, just a jog through the neighborhood to raise funds for a charity. Not being the wisest of runners, I started off at an impossible pace. Within a mile I was sucking air. At the right time, however, the spectators encouraged me. Sympathetic onlookers urged me on. One compassionate lady passed out cups of water, another sprayed us down with a hose. I had never seen these people, but that didn't matter. I needed a voice of encouragement, and they gave it. Bolstered by their assurance, I kept going.

What if in the toughest steps of the race, I had heard words of accusation and not encouragement? And what if the accusations came not from strangers I could dismiss but from my neighbors and family?

How would you like somebody to yell these words at you as you ran:

"Hey, liar! Why don't you do something honest with your life?" (see John 7:12).

"Here comes the foreigner. Why don't you go home where you belong?" (see John 8:48).

"Since when do they let children of the devil enter the race?" (see John 8:48).

That's what happened to Jesus. His own family called him a lunatic. His neighbors treated him even worse. When Jesus returned to his hometown, they tried to throw him off a cliff (Luke 4:29). But Jesus didn't quit running. Temptations didn't deter him. Accusations didn't defeat him. Nor did shame dishearten him. (From *Just Like Jesus* by Max Lucado)

REACTION

6. Which of the temptations faced by Christ would have been the most difficult for you to resist?

7. Theologians like to argue about whether Christ could have actually given in to the devil's temptations. Some argue that Jesus was divine, and God is incapable of evil. Others say if it was impossible for him to give in, then this temptation account is meaningless. What do you say?

8. Why is knowing, remembering, and clinging to God's Word so essential in overcoming temptation?

9. Are there times in your life in which you find yourself more susceptible and vulnerable to temptation than normal?

10. Following this temptation, Jesus officially began his ministry by selecting some followers. Jewish rabbis (i.e. teachers) customarily chose the brightest and most learned young men from their rabbinical schools as their disciples. Jesus, on the contrary, picked a few unlearned fishermen. What does this tell you about Christ?

11. Given the positive evidence you've just studied in Matthew 3 and 4, it's hard to imagine that anyone could become unhappy with Jesus. What about his flawless life and teaching would eventually create such controversy and animosity?

LIFE LESSONS

We can find great comfort and help in Matthew's account of Christ's temptation. Theological possibilities aside, the fact remains that in his humanity, Jesus was ravenous and exhausted, and the devil slyly moved in to try to exploit his vulnerable condition. Nothing in the text suggests there were only three temptations and that this encounter with Satan was a quick, five-minute ordeal. Satan's wilderness attack was tricky and relentless. But Christ resisted, meaning we have a victorious Savior who knows—really understands—what it is like to be wooed and enticed to do evil. And in the Lord's dogged adherence to God's truth, we have a magnificent example for what to do when we find ourselves "wanting to please our sinful selves, wanting the sinful things we see, and being too proud of what we have" (1 John 2:16 NCV).

DEVOTION

Thank you, Lord, that you understand our weaknesses. While on earth, you were tempted in every way that we are. Praise you, Lord, for your steadfast refusal to sin. You are holy, and you have promised to make me holy. Grant me discernment today. Fill me with your all-powerful Spirit.

For more Bible passages on temptation, see 1 Corinthians 10:13; Hebrews 4:14–16; and James 1:12–15.

To complete the book of Matthew during this twelve-part study, read Matthew 3:1–4:25.

JOURNALING

Regarding the most common temptation in my life just now, some practical and specific steps I can take to combat its power are . . .

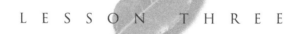

LESSON THREE

POWER IN
PRAYER

MAX
LUCADO

REFLECTION

In an intriguing cover story a few years back, a major news magazine disclosed that roughly four out of five adults say they pray at least once a week. The survey also revealed that 85 percent of those who pray claim they do *not* regularly receive answers to their prayers. How do you explain this contrast?

SITUATION

Having been introduced by Matthew as the long-awaited Messiah-King sent by God, Jesus sets forth the standards of his kingdom in the famous Sermon on the Mount. The ability to pray effectively is among the God-honoring practices expected of those who follow Christ.

OBSERVATION

Read Matthew 6:5–15 from the NCV or the NKJV.

NCV

⁵*"When you pray, don't be like the hypocrites. They love to stand in the synagogues and on the street corners and pray so people will see them. I tell you the truth, they already have their full reward. ⁶When you pray, you should go into your room and close the door and pray to your Father who cannot be seen. Your Father can see what is done in secret, and he will reward you.*

⁷*"And when you pray, don't be like those people who don't know God. They continue saying things that mean nothing, thinking that God will hear them because of their many words. ⁸Don't be like them, because your Father knows the things you need before you ask him. ⁹So when you pray, you should pray like this:*

'Our Father in heaven,

may your name always be kept holy.

*10*May your kingdom come

and what you want be done,

here on earth as it is in heaven.

*11*Give us the food we need for each day.

*12*Forgive us for our sins,

just as we have forgiven those who sinned against us.

*13*And do not cause us to be tempted,

but save us from the Evil One.'

14"Yes, if you forgive others for their sins, your Father in heaven will also forgive you for your sins. *15*But if you don't forgive others, your Father in heaven will not forgive your sins."

NKJV

5"And when you pray, you shall not be like the hypocrites. For they love to pray standing in the synagogues and on the corners of the streets, that they may be seen by men. Assuredly, I say to you, they have their reward. *6*But you, when you pray, go into your room, and when you have shut your door, pray to your Father who is in the secret place; and your Father who sees in secret will reward you openly. *7*And when you pray, do not use vain repetitions as the heathen do. For they think that they will be heard for their many words.

8"Therefore do not be like them. For your Father knows the things you have need of before you ask Him. *9*In this manner, therefore, pray:

Our Father in heaven,

Hallowed be Your name.

10 Your kingdom come.

Your will be done

On earth as it is in heaven.

11 Give us this day our daily bread.

*12*And forgive us our debts,

As we forgive our debtors.

*13*And do not lead us into temptation,

But deliver us from the evil one.

For Yours is the kingdom and the power and the glory forever. Amen.

14"For if you forgive men their trespasses, your heavenly Father will also forgive you. *15*But if you do not forgive men their trespasses, neither will your Father forgive your trespasses."

EXPLORATION

1. How did Jesus describe the prayer habits of the religious "hypocrites"?

2. What did Jesus say about repetitive or "wordy" prayers?

3. Why did Jesus instruct his followers to address God as Father and not with some other title or form of address?

4. Before asking God for needs and desires, what kinds of things are we commanded by Christ to express?

5. How is a forgiving spirit connected to effective praying?

INSPIRATION

Do this. Change your definition of prayer. Think of prayers less as an activity for God and more as an awareness of God. Seek to live in uninterrupted awareness. Acknowledge his presence everywhere you go. As you stand in line to register your car, think, *Thank you, Lord, for being here.* In the grocery as you shop, *Your presence, my King, I welcome.* As you wash the dishes, worship your Maker. Brother Lawrence did. This well-known saint called himself the "lord of pots and pans." In his book *The Practice of the Presence of God*, he wrote:

> The time of business does not with me differ from the time of prayer;
> and in the noise and clatter of my kitchen, while several persons are
> at the same time calling for different things, I possess God in as great
> tranquility as if I were upon my knees at the blessed sacrament.

Though a rookie in the League of Unceasing Prayer, I sure enjoy the pursuit. I've discovered the strength of carrying on two conversations: one with a person, another with the Person. One can, at once, listen and petition. As a person unfolds his problem, I'm often silently saying, *God, a little help here, please.* He always provides it . . . Throughout the day, my thoughts are marked with phrases: *Guide me, dear Father. Forgive that idea, please. Protect my daughters today.* (From *Come Thirsty* by Max Lucado)

REACTION

6. Do you think in those terms—of prayer as an awareness of God that results in an ongoing conversation with God (1 Thess. 5:17)? If not, what are your greatest impediments to a more consistent prayer life?

7. Jesus observed that much prayer is inauthentic and for show. How much "bogus" praying goes on in churches? In your life?

8. Look again at the specific sequence of prayer Jesus advocated. What is significant about this more God-centered way of praying?

9. Mark 1:35 and Luke 6:12 give us a window into Christ's personal discipline of prayer. What are the implications for us based on Christ's example here?

10. What other factors make us effective in prayer? (See Luke 18:1–8 for one example.)

11. Do you find you easily get distracted when you pray? Why do you think that is?

LIFE LESSONS

Countless Christians have been strengthened in the area of prayer by learning to follow the A-C-T-S acronym. The A refers to *adoration*, in which one spends a few moments focusing on the nature of God (his holiness, power, mercy, goodness, etc.) and praising him for who he is. The C stands for *confession*. Here, a believer, with the help of the Spirit, acknowledges personal failings (1 John 1:9) and claims the endless forgiveness of God. The T reminds us to engage in *thanksgiving*, expressing appreciation and gratitude for all of God's many blessing—spiritual and material. The S of A-C-T-S is a call to *supplication*, that is, asking God to supply our needs and the needs of others (for power, endurance, wisdom, financial and relational help, and so on). Try this for the next few days during your commute, exercise, or other activities in your daily routine.

DEVOTION

Lord, give me a heart that hungers for you. I ask the same thing your original disciples asked, "Teach me to pray"—in faith, with boldness, and in accordance with your perfect will. Help me to see prayer, not as a dry duty, but as an opportunity to commune with you, all day every day.

For more Bible passages on prayer, see Nehemiah 1:4–11; John 17:1–26; Ephesians 6:18; and Philippians 4:6–7.

To complete the book of Matthew during this twelve-part study, read Matthew 5:1–7:29.

JOURNALING

Make up a prayer list. Write down five God-honoring things you'd like to see the Lord do:

- in your own heart/life
- in your marriage/family
- in your church
- at work
- in the world

LESSON FOUR

THE
COMPASSION
OF CHRIST

MAX
LUCADO

REFLECTION

In her spiritual memoir, author Anne Lamott describes the man who was instrumental in her conversion by saying, "He was about the first Christian I ever met whom I could stand to be in the same room with. Most Christians seemed almost hostile in their belief that they were saved and you weren't" (Anne Lamott, *Traveling Mercies: Some Thoughts on Faith*, [New York: Anchor, 1999], 43). Why do so many irreligious people feel this way about church and about Christians?

SITUATION

Having focused on Christ's words (i.e., the Sermon on the Mount in chapters 5–7), Matthew next shines his spotlight on Christ's works. Through assorted miracles and in his relentless concern for empty, hurting people, Jesus consistently displays divine compassion. Jesus' acts of mercy only accentuate the heartless indifference Israel's religious leaders show toward the plight of the people.

OBSERVATION

Read Matthew 9:18–38 from the NCV or the NKJV.

NCV

¹⁸*While Jesus was saying these things, a leader of the synagogue came to him. He bowed down before Jesus and said, "My daughter has just died. But if you come and lay your hand on her, she will live again." ¹⁹So Jesus and his followers stood up and went with the leader.*

²⁰*Then a woman who had been bleeding for twelve years came behind Jesus and touched the edge of his coat. ²¹She was thinking, "If I can just touch his clothes, I will be healed."*

²²*Jesus turned and saw the woman and said, "Be encouraged, dear woman. You are made well because you believed." And the woman was healed from that moment on.*

²³*Jesus continued along with the leader and went into his house. There he saw the funeral musicians and many people crying. ²⁴Jesus said, "Go away. The girl is not dead, only asleep." But the people laughed at him. ²⁵After the crowd had been thrown out of the house, Jesus went into the girl's room and took hold of her hand, and she stood up.*

²⁶The news about this spread all around the area.

²⁷When Jesus was leaving there, two blind men followed him. They cried out, "Have mercy on us, Son of David!"

²⁸After Jesus went inside, the blind men went with him. He asked the men, "Do you believe that I can make you see again?"

They answered, "Yes, Lord."

²⁹Then Jesus touched their eyes and said, "Because you believe I can make you see again, it will happen." ³⁰Then the men were able to see. But Jesus warned them strongly, saying, "Don't tell anyone about this." ³¹But the blind men left and spread the news about Jesus all around that area.

³²When the two men were leaving, some people brought another man to Jesus. This man could not talk because he had a demon in him. ³³After Jesus forced the demon to leave the man, he was able to speak. The crowd was amazed and said, "We have never seen anything like this in Israel."

³⁴But the Pharisees said, "The prince of demons is the one that gives him power to force demons out."

³⁵Jesus traveled through all the towns and villages, teaching in their synagogues, preaching the Good News about the kingdom, and healing all kinds of diseases and sicknesses. ³⁶When he saw the crowds, he felt sorry for them because they were hurting and helpless, like sheep without a shepherd. ³⁷Jesus said to his followers, "There are many people to harvest but only a few workers to help harvest them. ³⁸Pray to the Lord, who owns the harvest, that he will send more workers to gather his harvest."

NKJV

¹⁸While He spoke these things to them, behold, a ruler came and worshiped Him, saying, "My daughter has just died, but come and lay Your hand on her and she will live." ¹⁹So Jesus arose and followed him, and so did His disciples.

²⁰And suddenly, a woman who had a flow of blood for twelve years came from behind and touched the hem of His garment. ²¹For she said to herself, "If only I may touch His garment, I shall be made well." ²²But Jesus turned around, and when He saw her He said, "Be of good cheer, daughter; your faith has made you well." And the woman was made well from that hour.

²³When Jesus came into the ruler's house, and saw the flute players and the noisy crowd wailing, ²⁴He said to them, "Make room, for the girl is not dead, but sleeping." And they ridiculed Him. ²⁵But when the crowd was put outside, He went in and took her by the hand, and the girl arose. ²⁶And the report of this went out into all that land.

²⁷When Jesus departed from there, two blind men followed Him, crying out and saying, "Son of David, have mercy on us!"

²⁸And when He had come into the house, the blind men came to Him. And Jesus said to them, "Do you believe that I am able to do this?"

They said to Him, "Yes, Lord."

29Then He touched their eyes, saying, "According to your faith let it be to you." 30And their eyes were opened. And Jesus sternly warned them, saying, "See that no one knows it." 31But when they had departed, they spread the news about Him in all that country.

32As they went out, behold, they brought to Him a man, mute and demon-possessed. 33And when the demon was cast out, the mute spoke. And the multitudes marveled, saying, "It was never seen like this in Israel!"

34But the Pharisees said, "He casts out demons by the ruler of the demons."

35Then Jesus went about all the cities and villages, teaching in their synagogues, preaching the gospel of the kingdom, and healing every sickness and every disease among the people. 36But when He saw the multitudes, He was moved with compassion for them, because they were weary and scattered, like sheep having no shepherd. 37Then He said to His disciples, "The harvest truly is plentiful, but the laborers are few. 38Therefore pray the Lord of the harvest to send out laborers into His harvest."

EXPLORATION

1. In rapid-fire succession, Jesus performed a series of healing miracles. What were they?

2. What role did faith play in these people's experiences of Christ's power?

3. What unusual or surprising command did Jesus give the blind men he healed? Why did they disobey?

4. How does the "official" response of Israel's religious leaders to Christ's healing ministry compare to the response of the masses?

5. What specific factors does Matthew say elicited Christ's compassion?

INSPIRATION

They were like sheep without a shepherd. So he began teaching them many things (Mark 6:34 NCV).

When Jesus landed and saw a large crowd, he had compassion on them and healed their sick (Matt. 14:14 NIV).

It's a good thing those verses weren't written about me.

It's a good thing thousands of people weren't depending on Max for their teaching and nourishment. Especially on a day when I'd just heard of the death of a dear friend . . . Especially after I'd gotten into a boat to escape the crowds. Had that been me in Jesus' sandals on that Bethsaida beach, the verses would read something like:

They were like sheep without a shepherd. So Max told them to quit grazing on his pasture and to head back to their pens.

When Max landed and saw a large crowd, he mumbled something about how hard it was to get a day off and radioed for the helicopter. Then he and the disciples escaped to a private retreat.

It's a good thing I wasn't responsible for those people. I would have been in no mood to teach them, no mood to help them. I would have had no desire even to be with them.

But, as I think about it, Jesus had no desire to be with them either . . . What made him change his mind and spend the day with the people he was trying to avoid?

Answer? Take a look at five words in Matthew 14:14:

"He had compassion on them."

The Greek word used for compassion in this passage is *splanchnizomai*, which won't mean much to you unless you are in the health professions and studied "splanchnology" in school. If so, you remember that "splanchnology" is a study of the visceral parts. Or, in contemporary jargon, a study of the gut.

When Matthew writes that Jesus had compassion on the people, he is not saying that Jesus felt casual pity for them. No, the term is far more graphic. Matthew is saying that Jesus felt their hurt in his gut:

- He felt the limp of the crippled.

- He felt the hurt of the diseased.

- He felt the loneliness of the leper.

- He felt the embarrassment of the sinful.

And once he felt their hurts, he couldn't help but heal their hurts. He was moved in the stomach by their needs. He was so touched by their needs that he forgot his own needs. He was so moved by the people's hurts that he put his hurts on the back burner. (From *In the Eye of the Storm* by Max Lucado)

REACTION

6. How would you define compassion in your own words?

7. What does this series of incidents reveal to you about the heart of Jesus?

8. The picture that all of the Gospels paint of the Pharisees, scribes, and teachers of the law is of a dour, disapproving bunch. What prompts such a petty response in the face of God's mercy and grace?

9. What are some specific things the Church could do to correct its reputation for being harsh and hostile?

10. When was the last time you felt torn up inside over the plight of someone else? What did you do?

11. How does a Christian become more compassionate? Is it actually possible to develop this quality—or is this more an issue of one's temperament?

LIFE LESSONS

The clear testimony of Scripture, both Old and New Testaments, is that God aches when his people hurt (see Exodus 2:23–25). He enters into our suffering, identifying fully with us in our pain. But more than just experiencing emotions of pity and sorrow, compelled by his compassion, God acts (see Exodus 3:1–10). There is no better demonstration of this than Christ. His whole ministry reveals this deep concern in the heart of God that relentlessly goes to any length to bring comfort. As followers of Jesus, as those engaged in the lifelong process of becoming like him, we must demonstrate this same kind of active compassion in an ever-increasing way.

DEVOTION

Lord Jesus, your heart overflows with an aching desire to find and help those who hurt. Thank you for loving me with such deep tenderness. Show me how to be more caring and compassionate in my daily life. May your gentle concern flow through me. May I be a healing presence to those around me.

For more Bible passages on compassion, see Psalm 103; Psalm 116:5; Isaiah 49:13; Luke 15:20; and Colossians 3:12.

To complete the book of Matthew during this twelve-part study, read Matthew 8:1–9:38.

JOURNALING

Who are the top candidates in your life for God's compassion today? List them and, while listening to the Spirit, brainstorm some specific steps you could take to show Christlike concern.

LESSON FIVE

FOLLOWING CHRIST

MAX LUCADO

REFLECTION

The so-called health-and-wealth gospel says that because Christians are the "King's kids," we are entitled to a life of abundance and blessing. If we'll just live by faith, we'll be immune from disaster and distress. We'll experience favor from both God and men. What do you think about such "prosperity" teaching? Is it biblical? Why or why not?

SITUATION

Conventional wisdom during the time of Christ said that people only suffered as a result of divine punishment. Got difficulty in your life? Hey, that's conclusive proof that you must not be living in a way that pleases God. Jesus torpedoed this kind of thinking by letting his followers know that they should expect a life of persecution. Obedience to Christ will bring trouble from the world.

OBSERVATION

Read Matthew 10:24–42 from the NCV or the NKJV.

NCV

24"A student is not better than his teacher, and a servant is not better than his master. 25A student should be satisfied to become like his teacher; a servant should be satisfied to become like his master. If the head of the family is called Beelzebul, then the other members of the family will be called worse names!

26"So don't be afraid of those people, because everything that is hidden will be shown. Everything that is secret will be made known. 27I tell you these things in the dark, but I want you to tell them in the light. What you hear whispered in your ear you should shout from the housetops. 28Don't be afraid of people, who can kill the body but cannot kill the soul. The only one you should fear is the one who can destroy the soul and the body in hell. 29Two sparrows cost only a penny, but not even one of them can die without your Father's knowing it. 30God even knows how many hairs are on your head.

³¹"So don't be afraid. You are worth much more than many sparrows.

³²"All those who stand before others and say they believe in me, I will say before my Father in heaven that they belong to me. ³³But all who stand before others and say they do not believe in me, I will say before my Father in heaven that they do not belong to me.

³⁴"Don't think that I came to bring peace to the earth. I did not come to bring peace, but a sword. ³⁵I have come so that

'a son will be against his father,

a daughter will be against her mother,

a daughter-in-law will be against her mother-in-law.

³⁶A person's enemies will be members of his own family.'

³⁷"Those who love their father or mother more than they love me are not worthy to be my followers. Those who love their son or daughter more than they love me are not worthy to be my followers. ³⁸Whoever is not willing to carry the cross and follow me is not worthy of me. ³⁹Those who try to hold on to their lives will give up true life. Those who give up their lives for me will hold on to true life. ⁴⁰Whoever accepts you also accepts me, and whoever accepts me also accepts the One who sent me. ⁴¹Whoever meets a prophet and accepts him will receive the reward of a prophet. And whoever accepts a good person because that person is good will receive the reward of a good person. ⁴²Those who give one of these little ones a cup of cold water because they are my followers will truly get their reward."

NKJV

²⁴"A disciple is not above his teacher, nor a servant above his master. ²⁵It is enough for a disciple that he be like his teacher, and a servant like his master. If they have called the master of the house Beelzebub, how much more will they call those of his household! ²⁶Therefore do not fear them. For there is nothing covered that will not be revealed, and hidden that will not be known.

²⁷"Whatever I tell you in the dark, speak in the light; and what you hear in the ear, preach on the housetops. ²⁸And do not fear those who kill the body but cannot kill the soul. But rather fear Him who is able to destroy both soul and body in hell. ²⁹Are not two sparrows sold for a copper coin? And not one of them falls to the ground apart from your Father's will. ³⁰But the very hairs of your head are all numbered. ³¹Do not fear therefore; you are of more value than many sparrows.

³²"Therefore whoever confesses Me before men, him I will also confess before My Father who is in heaven. ³³But whoever denies Me before men, him I will also deny before My Father who is in heaven.

³⁴"Do not think that I came to bring peace on earth. I did not come to bring peace but a sword. ³⁵For I have come to 'set a man against his father, a daughter against her mother, and a daughter-in-law against her mother-in-law'; ³⁶and 'a man's enemies will be those of his own household.'

[37]*"He who loves father or mother more than Me is not worthy of Me. And he who loves son or daughter more than Me is not worthy of Me.* [38]*And he who does not take his cross and follow after Me is not worthy of Me.* [39]*He who finds his life will lose it, and he who loses his life for My sake will find it.*

[40]*"He who receives you receives Me, and he who receives Me receives Him who sent Me.* [41]*He who receives a prophet in the name of a prophet shall receive a prophet's reward. And he who receives a righteous man in the name of a righteous man shall receive a righteous man's reward.* [42]*And whoever gives one of these little ones only a cup of cold water in the name of a disciple, assuredly, I say to you, he shall by no means lose his reward."*

EXPLORATION

1. What is the disturbing "promise" of Christ in verses 24 and 25?

2. Why does Jesus suggest it is foolish to be afraid of people?

3. What examples does Jesus use to convey the idea that God really is looking out for us?

4. What rewards does Christ promise in this passage to those who faithfully follow him?

5. Looking back over this section, do you find it more disturbing or more comforting? Why?

INSPIRATION

The story is told of a man on an African safari deep in the jungle. The guide before him had a machete and was whacking away the tall weeds and thick underbrush. The traveler, wearied and hot, asked in frustration, "Where are we? Do you know where you are taking me? Where is the path?!" The seasoned guide stopped and looked back at the man and replied, "I am the path."

We ask the same questions, don't we? We ask God, "Where are you taking me? Where is the path?" And he, like the guide, doesn't tell us. Oh, he may give us a hint or two, but that's all. If he did, would we understand? Would we comprehend our location? No, like the traveler, we are unacquainted with this jungle. So rather than give us an answer, Jesus gives us a far greater gift. He gives us himself.

Does he remove the jungle? No, the vegetation is still thick.

Does he purge the predators? No, danger still lurks. Jesus doesn't give hope by changing the jungle; he restores our hope by giving us himself. And he has promised to stay until the very end. *"I am with you always, to the very end of the age"* (Matt. 28:20 NIV).

We need that reminder. We all need that reminder. For all of us need hope.

Some of you don't need it right now. Your jungle has become a meadow and your journey a delight. If such is the case, congratulations. But remember—we do not know what tomorrow holds. We do not know where this road will lead. You may be one turn from a cemetery, from a hospital bed, from an empty house. You may be a bend in the road from a jungle. (From *Traveling Light* by Max Lucado)

REACTION

6. Does following Christ ever feel like that to you—like hacking your way through a wild jungle, with no clear sense of direction?

7. Given these stark and sobering words of Christ, what kind of reception should we expect as we live out our faith in the world, at work, in the neighborhood, at school?

8. What are some specific ways a follower of Jesus can acknowledge him before other people?

9. What do you think Jesus means when he speaks of losing one's life for Christ's sake? It sounds radical and scary. What does this look like in everyday terms?

10. What have been the highlights and lowlights in your time as a follower of Jesus?

11. What are your most consistent struggles in trying to walk with Christ on a daily basis?

LIFE LESSONS

We need to remember that the first disciples were ordinary men called to an extraordinary mission. Before we turned them into stain-glassed saints in the windows of our cathedrals, Peter, John, and all the rest were just regular guys, trying to make a living, trying to get along in life. They weren't seminary grads or spiritual giants. They didn't possess superhuman qualities. The most we can say about them is that their devotion to Jesus outweighed—by a hair—their fears and insecurities. As a result, God changed them and used them to accomplish some mind-boggling things. Why couldn't God—why wouldn't God—do the same thing in and through you and me?

DEVOTION

Lord, you haven't called me to a life of ease and comfort. You have called me to a life of trust and obedience. Help me to grow in you. And help me resist the common but erroneous notion that following you will be anything but hard.

For more Bible passages on what it means to follow Christ, see Psalm 15; Mark 8:34; Luke 14:25–35; and 2 Timothy 2:1–7.

To complete the book of Matthew during this twelve-part study, read Matthew 10:1–42.

JOURNALING

What are your biggest struggles just now? In light of what you've just studied, how might God be working despite your troubles?

LESSON SIX

HEAVEN'S
GREAT
INVITATION

MAX
LUCADO

REFLECTION

Invitations to join this club or that . . . requests for our presence at a party this
weekend or a wedding next month . . . proposals for a deal here or a partnership
there . . . face it, life is filled with offers. What are some of the best invitations
you've ever received? What have been the worst?

SITUATION

Ever since the time of Moses, Israel had been in possession of God's law, includ-
ing his clear-cut commands and provisions for the Sabbath, the weekly day of
rest and reflection. Over the centuries, the Jewish leaders had turned it all into a
confusing, soul-destroying system. Enter Jesus with a startling invitation . . .

OBSERVATION

Read Matthew 11:20–30 from the NCV or the NKJV.

NCV

20 Then Jesus criticized the cities where he did most of his miracles, because the people did not change their lives and stop sinning. 21 He said, "How terrible for you, Korazin! How terrible for you, Bethsaida! If the same miracles I did in you had happened in Tyre and Sidon, those people would have changed their lives a long time ago. They would have worn rough cloth and put ashes on themselves to show they had changed. 22 But I tell you, on the Judgment Day it will be better for Tyre and Sidon than for you. 23 And you, Capernaum, will you be lifted up to heaven? No, you will be thrown down to the depths. If the miracles I did in you had happened in Sodom, its people would have stopped sinning, and it would still be a city today. 24 But I tell you, on the Judgment Day it will be better for Sodom than for you."

25 At that time Jesus said, "I praise you, Father, Lord of heaven and earth, because you have hidden these things from the people who are wise and smart. But you have shown them to those who are like little children. 26 Yes, Father, this is what you really wanted.

27 "My Father has given me all things. No one knows the Son, except the Father. And no one knows the Father, except the Son and those whom the Son chooses to tell.

28 "Come to me, all of you who are tired and have heavy loads, and I will give you rest. 29 Accept my teachings and learn from me, because I am gentle and humble in spirit, and you will find rest for your lives. 30 The teaching that I ask you to accept is easy; the load I give you to carry is light."

NKJV

20 Then He began to rebuke the cities in which most of His mighty works had been done, because they did not repent: 21 "Woe to you, Chorazin! Woe to you, Bethsaida! For if the mighty works which were done in you had been done in Tyre and Sidon, they would have repented long ago in sackcloth and ashes. 22 But I say to you, it will be more tolerable for Tyre and Sidon in the day of judgment than for you. 23 And you, Capernaum, who are exalted to heaven, will be brought down to Hades; for if the mighty works which were done in you had been done in Sodom, it would have remained until this day. 24 But I say to you that it shall be more tolerable for the land of Sodom in the day of judgment than for you."

25 At that time Jesus answered and said, "I thank You, Father, Lord of heaven and earth, that You have hidden these things from the wise and prudent and have revealed them to babes. 26 Even so, Father, for so it seemed good in Your sight. 27 All things have been delivered to Me by My Father, and no one knows the Son except the Father. Nor does anyone know the Father except the Son, and the one to whom the Son wills to reveal Him. 28 Come to Me, all you who labor and are heavy laden, and I will give you rest. 29 Take My yoke upon you and learn from Me, for I am gentle and lowly in heart, and you will find rest for your souls. 30 For My yoke is easy and My burden is light."

EXPLORATION

1. Take a moment to consider the context of this passage. Then look back at verses 16–19. What do they reveal about human nature?

2. Why did Jesus denounce so many of the cities in which he had ministered?

3. What do you make of Jesus' prayer here? What is he really saying?

4. To whom does Christ extend his gracious invitation?

5. What does this invitation tell you about the heart of God?

INSPIRATION

Invitations. Words embossed on a letter: "You are invited to a gala celebrating the grand opening of . . ." Requests received in the mail: "Mr. and Mrs. John Smith request your presence at the wedding of their daughter . . ." Surprises over the phone: "Hey, Joe. I've got an extra ticket to the game. Interested?"

To receive an invitation is to be honored—to be held in high esteem. For that reason all invitations deserve a kind and thoughtful response.

But the most incredible invitations are not found in envelopes or fortune cookies, they are found in the Bible. You can't read about God without finding him issuing invitations. He invited Eve to marry Adam, the animals to enter the ark, David to be king, Israel to leave bondage, Nehemiah to rebuild Jerusalem. God is an inviting God. He invited Mary to birth his son, the disciples to fish for men, the adulterous woman to start over, and Thomas to touch his wounds. God is the King who prepares the palace, sets the table, and invites his subjects to come in.

In fact, it seems his favorite word is *come*.

"Come, let us talk about these things. Though your sins are like scarlet, they can be as white as snow" (Isa. 1:18, emphasis added).

"All you who are thirsty, come and drink" (Isa. 55:1 NCV, emphasis added).

"Come to me, all of you who are tired and have heavy loads, and I will give you rest" (Matt. 11:28 NCV, emphasis added).

"Come to the wedding feast" (Matt. 22:4 NCV, emphasis added).

"Come follow me, and I will make you fish for people" (Mark 1:17 NCV, emphasis added).

"Let anyone who is thirsty come to me and drink" (John 7:37 NCV, emphasis added).

God is a God who invites. God is a God who calls. God is a God who opens the door and waves his hand, pointing pilgrims to a full table.

His invitation is not just for a meal, however, it is for life. An invitation to come into his kingdom and take up residence in a tearless, graveless, painless world. Who can come? Whoever wishes. The invitation is at once universal and personal. (From *And the Angels Were Silent* by Max Lucado)

REACTION

6. What do you remember about the first time you ever comprehended and responded to Christ's invitation to come to him?

7. What is Jesus' yoke, and what does he mean when he says it is "easy"—easy compared to what?

8. In what ways do modern Christians (and churches) repeat the errors of the Pharisees and create a religious system that wears people out?

9. What sorts of daily burdens bring the most weariness to your soul?

10. When have you experienced genuine soul rest to the deepest degree? To what do you attribute this?

11. What counsel would you give to someone who said, "I'm at the end of my rope. I'm burned-out. Please, help me. Tell me what to do!"?

LIFE LESSONS

Christ looked into the leathery faces of farmers and weary faces of housewives and offered rest. The crowds came. They poured out of the cul-de-sacs and office complexes of their day. They brought him the burdens of their existence, and he gave them not religion, not doctrine, not systems, but rest. Today, Christ continues to look into the disillusioned eyes of the churchgoer, the cynical stare of a banker, and the hungry eyes of a bartender. And his paradoxical invitation still stands: "Take my yoke upon you and learn from me, for I am gentle and humble in heart, and you will find rest for your souls" (Matt. 11:29 NIV).

DEVOTION

Father, I want to trade my burdens—all my man-made rules and self-imposed religious obligations—for the true rest that Jesus promised. Thanks for the constant invitation to come to you. Grant me the wisdom and courage to live as you intended, so that I might attract others to you, and not repel them.

For more Bible passages on rest, see Exodus 23:12; Psalm 62; Isaiah 30:15; and Hebrews 4.

To complete the book of Matthew during this twelve-part study, read Matthew 11:1–12:50.

JOURNALING

How can you give all your worries to God (1 Pet. 5:7)? If you did this, how much more "restful," how much less anxious, would your soul be?

LESSON SEVEN

SPIRITUAL
RECEPTIVITY

MAX
LUCADO

REFLECTION

The Bible is filled with agricultural imagery. Ours is not the agrarian society it used to be, but spending on lawn-and-garden supplies has nevertheless sky-rocketed in recent years. If you have much experience growing flowers, fruit, or vegetables, what have you found is the secret to success in the yard or garden?

SITUATION

The kingdom of heaven was a source of great hope for the Jewish people. And yet this much-discussed subject was also a matter of major misunderstanding. Through short stories called parables, Jesus used common, everyday objects and activities to illustrate various truths about God's kingdom.

OBSERVATION

Read Matthew 13:3–23 from the NCV or the NKJV.

NCV

3Then Jesus used stories to teach them many things. He said: "A farmer went out to plant his seed. 4While he was planting, some seed fell by the road, and the birds came and ate it all up. 5Some seed fell on rocky ground, where there wasn't much dirt. That seed grew very fast, because the ground was not deep. 6But when the sun rose, the plants dried up, because they did not have deep roots. 7Some other seed fell among thorny weeds, which grew and choked the good plants. 8Some other seed fell on good ground where it grew and produced a crop. Some plants made a hundred times more, some made sixty times more, and some made thirty times more. 9You people who can hear me, listen."

10The followers came to Jesus and asked, "Why do you use stories to teach the people?"

11Jesus answered, "You have been chosen to know the secrets about the kingdom of heaven, but others cannot know these secrets. 12Those who have understanding will be given more, and they will have all they need. But those who do not have understanding, even what they have will be taken away from them. 13This is why I use stories to teach the people: They see, but they don't really see. They hear, but they don't really hear or understand. 14So they show that the things Isaiah said about them are true:

> *'You will listen and listen, but you will not understand.*
>
> *You will look and look, but you will not learn.*
>
> *15For the minds of these people have become stubborn.*
>
> *They do not hear with their ears,*
>
> *and they have closed their eyes.*
>
> *Otherwise they might really understand*
>
> *what they see with their eyes*
>
> *and hear with their ears.*
>
> *They might really understand in their minds*
>
> *and come back to me and be healed.'*

16But you are blessed, because you see with your eyes and hear with your ears. 17I tell you the truth, many prophets and good people wanted to see the things that you now see, but they did not see them. And they wanted to hear the things that you now hear, but they did not hear them.

18"So listen to the meaning of that story about the farmer. 19What is the seed that fell by the road? That seed is like the person who hears the message about the kingdom but does not understand it. The Evil One comes and takes away what was planted in that person's heart. 20And what is the seed that fell on rocky ground? That seed is like the person who hears the teaching and quickly accepts it with joy. 21But he does not let the teaching go deep into his life, so he keeps it only a short time. When trouble or persecution comes because of the teaching he accepted, he quickly gives up. 22And what is the seed that fell among the thorny weeds? That seed is like the person who hears the teaching but lets worries about this life and the temptation of wealth stop that teaching from growing. So the teaching does not produce fruit in that person's life. 23But what is the seed that fell on the good ground? That seed is like the person who hears the teaching and understands it. That person grows and produces fruit, sometimes a hundred times more, sometimes sixty times more, and sometimes thirty times more."

NKJV

³Then He spoke many things to them in parables, saying: "Behold, a sower went out to sow. ⁴And as he sowed, some seed fell by the wayside; and the birds came and devoured them. ⁵Some fell on stony places, where they did not have much earth; and they immediately sprang up because they had no depth of earth. ⁶But when the sun was up they were scorched, and because they had no root they withered away. ⁷And some fell among thorns, and the thorns sprang up and choked them. ⁸But others fell on good ground and yielded a crop: some a hundredfold, some sixty, some thirty. ⁹He who has ears to hear, let him hear!"

¹⁰And the disciples came and said to Him, "Why do You speak to them in parables?"

¹¹He answered and said to them, "Because it has been given to you to know the mysteries of the kingdom of heaven, but to them it has not been given. ¹²For whoever has, to him more will be given, and he will have abundance; but whoever does not have, even what he has will be taken away from him. ¹³Therefore I speak to them in parables, because seeing they do not see, and hearing they do not hear, nor do they understand. ¹⁴And in them the prophecy of Isaiah is fulfilled, which says:

'Hearing you will hear and shall not understand,

And seeing you will see and not perceive;

¹⁵For the hearts of this people have grown dull.

Their ears are hard of hearing,

And their eyes they have closed,

Lest they should see with their eyes and hear with their ears,

Lest they should understand with their hearts and turn,

So that I should heal them.'

¹⁶But blessed are your eyes for they see, and your ears for they hear; ¹⁷for assuredly, I say to you that many prophets and righteous men desired to see what you see, and did not see it, and to hear what you hear, and did not hear it.

¹⁸"Therefore hear the parable of the sower: ¹⁹When anyone hears the word of the kingdom, and does not understand it, then the wicked one comes and snatches away what was sown in his heart. This is he who received seed by the wayside. ²⁰But he who received the seed on stony places, this is he who hears the word and immediately receives it with joy; ²¹yet he has no root in himself, but endures only for a while. For when tribulation or persecution arises because of the word, immediately he stumbles. ²²Now he who received seed among the thorns is he who hears the word, and the cares of this world and the deceitfulness of riches choke the word, and he becomes unfruitful. ²³But he who received seed on the good ground is he who hears the word and understands it, who indeed bears fruit and produces: some a hundredfold, some sixty, some thirty."

EXPLORATION

1. What happened in the story of the seed-sowing farmer?

2. What factor(s) determined whether the seed bore fruit?

3. Why did Jesus say he relied so heavily on parables in his teaching?

4. How did Jesus explain to his followers the underlying meaning of the parable of the four soils?

5. According to Jesus, is it enough for a person to be exposed to the Word of God? Why or why not?

INSPIRATION

To the Hebrew mind, the heart is a freeway cloverleaf where all emotions and prejudices and wisdom converge. It is a switch house that receives freight cars loaded with moods, ideas, emotions, and convictions and puts them on the right track.

And just as a low-grade oil or alloyed gasoline would cause you to question the performance of a refinery, evil acts and impure thoughts cause us to question the condition of our hearts . . . The heart is the center of the spiritual life. If the fruit of a tree is bad, you don't try to fix the fruit; you treat the roots. And if a person's actions are evil, it's not enough to change habits; you have to go deeper. You have to go to the heart of the problem, which is the problem of the heart.

That is why the state of the heart is so critical. What's the state of yours?

When someone barks at you, do you bark back or bite your tongue? That depends on the state of your heart.

When your schedule is too tight or your to-do list too long, do you lose your cool or keep it? That depends on the state of your heart.

When you are offered a morsel of gossip marinated in slander, do you turn it down or pass it on? That depends on the state of your heart.

Do you see the bag lady on the street as a burden on society or as an opportunity for God? That, too, depends on the state of your heart.

The state of your heart dictates whether you harbor a grudge or give grace, seek self-pity or seek Christ, drink human misery or taste God's mercy.

No wonder, then, the wise man begs, *"Above all else, guard your heart"* (Prov. 4:23 NIV).

David's prayer should be ours: *"Create in me a pure heart, O God"* (Ps. 51:10 NIV).

And Jesus' statement rings true: "Blessed are the pure in heart, for they shall see God." (From *The Applause of Heaven* by Max Lucado)

REACTION

6. A thousand people can hear the same sermon and only five are really impacted and changed. What makes the difference?

7. Explain how the four soils differ.

8. If a person realizes the soil of his heart is not conducive to growth or that her life is barren of fruit, what is necessary for change? Be specific and practical.

9. What does fruitfulness and abundance look like in a life that is yielded to God?

10. Compare your life to the soils described by Jesus. Which are you?

11. How is wealth "deceitful"? How does a citizen of the kingdom of heaven guard against loving money in this life?

LIFE LESSONS

The kingdom of God has both a present and a future aspect. During his first coming, Jesus fulfilled the role of a suffering servant. Through his death on the cross, he defeated the kingdom of darkness and made it possible for sinners to be forgiven and brought into his spiritual kingdom. He currently rules quietly in the hearts of those who are responsive to him, those who collectively make up his church. But at his second coming, Christ will rule all things. His kingdom then will be visible and universal, and it will never end. By letting his Word take root in our hearts, we bear fruit for God. Through a kind of spiritual cultivation we are to watch over our souls, keeping them from becoming hard or hostile to the truth and rooting out any weeds of worldliness that can choke the fruit of righteousness.

DEVOTION

Father, protect me from the evil one. Keep me from spiritual indifference and shallowness. Make me aware and intolerant of worldly attitudes. Give me an ever-deepening desire to receive your word with great eagerness. May it take root deeply in my soul so that I bear lasting fruit for your glory.

For more Bible passages on fruitfulness, see Hosea 10:11–12; Luke 3:8–9; 13:6–9; John 15; Galatians 5:22–23; Colossians 1:10.

To complete the book of Matthew during this twelve-part study, read Matthew 13:1–52.

JOURNALING

What are the worries of this world that threaten to make you unfruitful in your faith?

LESSON EIGHT

BREAD OF
LIFE

MAX
LUCADO

REFLECTION

Food is such a dominant part of daily life. When it's missing, we notice! Think about a time when you've gone without food, either by choice or by necessity. Describe the experience of being hungry and then of being able to eat again.

SITUATION

Against the backdrop of Herod's unjust execution of John the Baptist, Matthew shows both the power and compassion of Jesus. The Carpenter King feeds a crowd of five thousand men (plus women and children) with five loaves and two fish. Next he walks on water to the astonishment of his followers.

OBSERVATION

Read Matthew 14:13–21 from the NCV or the NKJV.

NCV

13When Jesus heard what had happened to John, he left in a boat and went to a lonely place by himself. But the crowds heard about it and followed him on foot from the towns. 14When he arrived, he saw a great crowd waiting. He felt sorry for them and healed those who were sick.

15When it was evening, his followers came to him and said, "No one lives in this place, and it is already late. Send the people away so they can go to the towns and buy food for themselves."

16But Jesus answered, "They don't need to go away. You give them something to eat."

17They said to him, "But we have only five loaves of bread and two fish."

18Jesus said, "Bring the bread and the fish to me." 19Then he told the people to sit down on the grass. He took the five loaves and the two fish and, looking to heaven, he thanked God for the food. Jesus divided the bread and gave it to his followers, who gave it to the people. 20All the people ate and were satisfied. Then the followers filled twelve baskets with the leftover pieces of food. 21There were about five thousand men there who ate, not counting women and children.

NKJV

13When Jesus heard it, He departed from there by boat to a deserted place by Himself. But when the multitudes heard it, they followed Him on foot from the cities. 14And when Jesus went out He saw a great multitude; and He was moved with compassion for them, and healed their sick. 15When it was evening, His disciples came to Him, saying, "This is a deserted place, and the hour is already late. Send the multitudes away, that they may go into the villages and buy themselves food."

16But Jesus said to them, "They do not need to go away. You give them something to eat."

17And they said to Him, "We have here only five loaves and two fish."

18He said, "Bring them here to Me." 19Then He commanded the multitudes to sit down on the grass. And He took the five loaves and the two fish, and looking up to heaven, He blessed and broke and gave the loaves to the disciples; and the disciples gave to the multitudes. 20So they all ate and were filled, and they took up twelve baskets full of the fragments that remained. 21Now those who had eaten were about five thousand men, besides women and children.

EXPLORATION

1. What terrible news did Jesus receive at the beginning of this passage (see Matthew 14:1–12)?

2. What was Jesus' response to this report?

3. How did the masses react when Jesus left by boat?

4. What was the attitude and recommendation of Christ's disciples when the day had ended and the crowds were still there?

5. How did Jesus ultimately deal with the situation, all those hungry people who had followed him to a remote location?

INSPIRATION

The feeding of the five thousand . . . answers the question, What does God do when his children are weak?

If God ever needed an excuse to give up on people, he has one here. Surely God is going to banish these followers until they learn to believe.

Is that what he does? You decide. *"Then Jesus took the loaves of bread, thanked God for them, and gave them to the people who were sitting there. He did the same with the fish, giving as much as the people wanted"* (John 6:11 NCV).

When the disciples didn't pray, Jesus prayed. When the disciples didn't see God, Jesus sought God. When the disciples were weak, Jesus was strong. When the disciples had no faith, Jesus had faith. He thanked God . . . He ignored the clouds and found the ray and thanked God for it.

Look what he does next. *"Jesus divided the bread and gave it to his followers, who gave it to the people"* (Matt. 14:19 NCV).

Rather than punish the disciples, he employs them. There they go, passing out the bread they didn't request, enjoying the answer to the prayer they didn't even pray. If Jesus would have acted according to the faith of his disciples, the multitudes would have gone unfed. But he didn't, and he doesn't. God is true to us even when we forget him.

God's blessings are dispensed according to the riches of his grace, not according to the depth of our faith. *"If we are not faithful, he will still be faithful, because he cannot be false to himself"* (2 Tim. 2:13 NCV).

Why is that important to know? So you won't get cynical. Look around you. Aren't there more mouths than bread? Aren't there more wounds than physicians? Aren't there more who need the truth than those who tell it? Aren't there more churches asleep than churches afire?

So what do we do? Throw up our hands and walk away? Tell the world we can't help them? That's what the disciples wanted to do. Should we just give up . . . ? No, we don't give up. We look up. We trust. We believe. And our optimism is not hollow. Christ has proven worthy. He has shown that he never fails, though there is nothing but failure in us.

God is faithful even when his children are not. (From *A Gentle Thunder* by Max Lucado)

REACTION

6. John the Baptist and Jesus were both cousins and colleagues. Speculate on the emotional condition and the natural desires Jesus must have been feeling when he heard about John's brutal execution.

7. How does Jesus' response in this situation epitomize the notion of compassionate, selfless servanthood?

8. How and where do we find the capacity to give, serve, and be centered on others when we are battling our own trials and tragedies?

9. Summarize the overall reaction of the disciples to this series of incidents. Can you relate to their attitudes and actions?

10. There is a tension in this passage between Christ's constant desire to commune with his Father and the needs of the people around him. How do we balance these competing needs—our own souls for rest and replenishment and the endless demands (many legitimate) of others?

11. Verse 19 notes that Jesus directed the people to sit on the grass. Mark 6:39 adds the little detail that it was "green" grass. What does this often overlooked fact remind us about the one known as the Good Shepherd? (Hint: See Psalm 23).

LIFE LESSONS

Life is messy and hard. People are needy and demanding. We are called to lives of sacrifice and service. How do we pull it off? Like the disciples of old, we follow the one with all power and compassion. We look to him. We listen to him. We do whatever he tells us. Ultimately we trust him to work through us. Such a life is scary and uncertain. We will be tested and pulled. But in the end our faith will grow and the needs of others will be met. The one fact we must cling to? Jesus is the bread of God who comes down from heaven and gives life to the world (John 6:33).

DEVOTION

Lord Jesus, you are the Bread of Life who gives life to the world. Give me the good sense to feed on you daily, to draw my strength from you. You are the Good Shepherd. Grant me the courage to follow your example so that I might serve others and lead them to you.

For more Bible passages on spiritual food, see Exodus 16:1–35; Isaiah 25; John 4:31–34; 6:27; Hebrews 5:12–14.

To complete the book of Matthew during this twelve-part study, read Matthew 13:53–17:27.

JOURNALING

Someone wisely said, "You cannot impart what you do not possess." What do you need to do to become a more effective servant to others, a more compelling witness to the goodness of the Lord?

LESSON NINE

HUMILITY

MAX
LUCADO

REFLECTION

In 1997, two world-famous women died within a few days of each other. Princess Diana was best known for her beauty and flashy sense of style. Mother Teresa of Calcutta was hailed for her tireless service to the poorest of the poor in India. What admirable qualities did each of these two women possess?

SITUATION

During the time of Christ, Israel was under the authority of the Roman Empire. Honor, power, pride, prestige, acclaim—these were the dominant values of Rome. Not surprisingly, Jesus advocated and modeled a different value system. The ways of the world are not the ways of the kingdom of Christ.

OBSERVATION

Read Matthew 18:1–14 from the NCV or the NKJV.

NCV

1At that time the followers came to Jesus and asked, "Who is greatest in the kingdom of heaven?"

2Jesus called a little child to him and stood the child before his followers. 3Then he said, "I tell you the truth, you must change and become like little children. Otherwise, you will never enter the kingdom of heaven. 4The greatest person in the kingdom of heaven is the one who makes himself humble like this child.

5"Whoever accepts a child in my name accepts me. 6If one of these little children believes in me, and someone causes that child to sin, it would be better for that person to have a large stone tied around the neck and be drowned in the sea. 7How terrible for the people of the world because of the things that cause them to sin. Such things will happen, but how terrible for the one who causes them to happen!

⁸*If your hand or your foot causes you to sin, cut it off and throw it away. It is better for you to lose part of your body and live forever than to have two hands and two feet and be thrown into the fire that burns forever.* ⁹*If your eye causes you to sin, take it out and throw it away. It is better for you to have only one eye and live forever than to have two eyes and be thrown into the fire of hell.*

¹⁰*"Be careful. Don't think these little children are worth nothing. I tell you that they have angels in heaven who are always with my Father in heaven.*

¹²*"If a man has a hundred sheep but one of the sheep gets lost, he will leave the other ninety-nine on the hill and go to look for the lost sheep.* ¹³*I tell you the truth, he is happier about that one sheep than about the ninety-nine that were never lost.* ¹⁴*In the same way, your Father in heaven does not want any of these little children to be lost.*

NKJV

¹*At that time the disciples came to Jesus, saying, "Who then is greatest in the kingdom of heaven?"*

²*Then Jesus called a little child to Him, set him in the midst of them,* ³*and said, "Assuredly, I say to you, unless you are converted and become as little children, you will by no means enter the kingdom of heaven.* ⁴*Therefore whoever humbles himself as this little child is the greatest in the kingdom of heaven.* ⁵*Whoever receives one little child like this in My name receives Me.*

⁶*"Whoever causes one of these little ones who believe in Me to sin, it would be better for him if a millstone were hung around his neck, and he were drowned in the depth of the sea.* ⁷*Woe to the world because of offenses! For offenses must come, but woe to that man by whom the offense comes!*

⁸*"If your hand or foot causes you to sin, cut it off and cast it from you. It is better for you to enter into life lame or maimed, rather than having two hands or two feet, to be cast into the everlasting fire.* ⁹*And if your eye causes you to sin, pluck it out and cast it from you. It is better for you to enter into life with one eye, rather than having two eyes, to be cast into hell fire.*

¹⁰*"Take heed that you do not despise one of these little ones, for I say to you that in heaven their angels always see the face of My Father who is in heaven.* ¹¹*For the Son of Man has come to save that which was lost.*

¹²*"What do you think? If a man has a hundred sheep, and one of them goes astray, does he not leave the ninety-nine and go to the mountains to seek the one that is straying?* ¹³*And if he should find it, assuredly, I say to you, he rejoices more over that sheep than over the ninety-nine that did not go astray.* ¹⁴*Even so it is not the will of your Father who is in heaven that one of these little ones should perish.*

EXPLORATION

1. What topic were the disciples discussing and debating?

2. How did Jesus settle their dispute? What quality did he call for?

3. How specifically did Jesus inject an eternal perspective into this conversation?

4. According to Jesus, who is great in God's eyes?

5. How did Jesus illustrate the importance of "lowly" and "forgotten" people like children?

INSPIRATION

Deflating inflated egos is so important to God that he offers to help.

He helped me. I recently spent an autumn week on a book tour. We saw long lines and crowded stores. One person after another complimented me. For three days I bathed in the river of praise. I began to believe the accolades. *All these people can't be wrong. I must be God's gift to readers.* My chest puffed so much I could hardly see where to autograph the books. Why, had I been born two thousand years earlier, we might read the gospels of Matthew, Max, Luke, and John. About the time I wondered if the Bible needed another epistle, God shot an arrow of humility in my direction.

We were running late for an evening book signing, late because the afternoon book signing had seen such long lines. We expected the same at the next store. Concerned, we phoned ahead. "We are running behind. Tell all the people we'll arrive soon."

"No need to hurry," the store manager assured.

"What about the people?"

"Neither one seems to be in a hurry."

Neither one?

By the time we reached the store, thankfully, the crowd of two people had tripled to six. We had scheduled two hours for the signing; I needed ten minutes.

Self-conscious about sitting alone at the table, I peppered the last person with questions. We talked about her parents, school, Social Security number, favorite birthday party. Against my pleadings, she had to go. So I sat alone at the table. Big stack of Lucado books, no one in line.

I asked the store manager, "Did you advertise?"

"We did. More than usual." She walked off.

The next time she passed I asked, "Had other signings?"

"Yes, usually we have a great response," and kept going.

I signed all the books at my table. I signed all the Lucado books on the shelves. I signed Tom Clancy and John Grisham books. Finally a customer came to the table. "You write books?" he asked, picking up the new one.

"I do. Want me to sign it?"

"No thanks," he answered and left.

God hit his target. Lest I forget, my daily reading the next morning had this passage: "Do not be wise in your own eyes" (Prov. 3:7 NKJV).

When you're full of yourself, God can't fill you. (From *Cure for the Common Life* by Max Lucado)

REACTION

6. Why do we get so full of ourselves so often?

7. Describe humility and give some examples.

8. Our society is a bit different from the ancient Roman Empire. What are the dominant values that our neighbors and colleagues live by?

9. What are the risks of living humbly, of taking a page from Mother Teresa's book and showing extraordinary kindness to the "least of these"?

10. In *The Weight of Glory*, C. S. Lewis observed: "There are no ordinary people. You have never talked to a mere mortal. Nations, cultures, arts, civilisations—these are mortal, and their life is to ours as the life of a gnat. But it is immortals whom we joke with, work with, marry, snub, and exploit—immortal horrors or everlasting splendours." Why is it so difficult to remember this, to treat others—all others—with dignity and respect?

11. What are the dangers of pride? (See Proverbs 16:18.)

LIFE LESSONS

We will either take our cues from the world or the Word. There are no other options. We can buy into the dominant temporal value system that says: *Be cutthroat. Compete. See all others as rivals. Promote yourself (by tearing others down). Pursue the acclaim of others.* Or we can embrace the rare and precious eternal value system that says: *Be Christ-like. Submit. See others as those whom you can serve. Live to promote Christ. Pursue the commendation of God.* The first way is the way of pride. The second way is the way of humility. The first way ends ironically in destruction. The second way culminates in exaltation.

DEVOTION

Lord, give me a discerning spirit and the transformed mind-set necessary to see that things are not what they appear. Help me to say no to the constant temptation to promote myself. Remind me constantly that my calling is to promote you and that I do this by serving others using the gifts and opportunities you give.

For more Bible passages on humility, see Psalm 18:27; Proverbs 11:2; 29:23; James 4:10; and 1 Peter 3:8.

To complete the book of Matthew during this twelve-part study, read Matthew 18:1–35.

JOURNALING

Make a short list of people God is nudging you to serve and some concrete ways you can do so.

MISSING THE MESSIAH

MAX LUCADO

REFLECTION

Disappointment always stems from unmet expectations. Our level of disappointment in any situation is directly tied to the difference between what we hoped for and what actually happened. Share some of your biggest disappointments or letdowns in life.

SITUATION

Jesus entered Jerusalem as a king . . . but not the exalted monarch many would have preferred. He rode a humble donkey, not the white horse of a conqueror. Dismounting, he promptly caused a scene at the temple, incurring the wrath of Israel's religious leaders. These head-scratching events coupled with all Jesus' other odd sayings and unusual views caused many to doubt his messianic claims.

OBSERVATION

Read Matthew 21:1–17 from the NCV or the NKJV.

NCV

¹As Jesus and his followers were coming closer to Jerusalem, they stopped at Bethphage at the hill called the Mount of Olives. From there Jesus sent two of his followers ²and said to them, "Go to the town you can see there. When you enter it, you will quickly find a donkey tied there with its colt. Untie them and bring them to me. ³If anyone asks you why you are taking the donkeys, say that the Master needs them, and he will send them at once."

⁴This was to bring about what the prophet had said:

⁵"Tell the people of Jerusalem,

'Your king is coming to you.

He is gentle and riding on a donkey,

on the colt of a donkey.'"

⁶*The followers went and did what Jesus told them to do. ⁷They brought the donkey and the colt to Jesus and laid their coats on them, and Jesus sat on them. ⁸Many people spread their coats on the road. Others cut branches from the trees and spread them on the road. ⁹The people were walking ahead of Jesus and behind him, shouting,*

"Praise to the Son of David!

God bless the One who comes in the name of the Lord!

Praise to God in heaven!"

¹⁰*When Jesus entered Jerusalem, all the city was filled with excitement. The people asked, "Who is this man?"*

¹¹*The crowd said, "This man is Jesus, the prophet from the town of Nazareth in Galilee."*

¹²*Jesus went into the Temple and threw out all the people who were buying and selling there. He turned over the tables of those who were exchanging different kinds of money, and he upset the benches of those who were selling doves. ¹³Jesus said to all the people there, "It is written in the Scriptures, 'My Temple will be called a house for prayer.' But you are changing it into a 'hideout for robbers.'"*

¹⁴*The blind and crippled people came to Jesus in the Temple, and he healed them. ¹⁵The leading priests and the teachers of the law saw that Jesus was doing wonderful things and that the children were praising him in the Temple, saying, "Praise to the Son of David." All these things made the priests and the teachers of the law very angry.*

¹⁶*They asked Jesus, "Do you hear the things these children are saying?"*

Jesus answered, "Yes. Haven't you read in the Scriptures, 'You have taught children and babies to sing praises'?"

¹⁷*Then Jesus left and went out of the city to Bethany, where he spent the night.*

NKJV

¹*Now when they drew near Jerusalem, and came to Bethphage, at the Mount of Olives, then Jesus sent two disciples, ²saying to them, "Go into the village opposite you, and immediately you will find a donkey tied, and a colt with her. Loose them and bring them to Me. ³And if anyone says anything to you, you shall say, 'The Lord has need of them,' and immediately he will send them."*

⁴*All this was done that it might be fulfilled which was spoken by the prophet, saying:*

⁵*"Tell the daughter of Zion,*

'Behold, your King is coming to you,

Lowly, and sitting on a donkey,

A colt, the foal of a donkey.'"

⁶*So the disciples went and did as Jesus commanded them. ⁷They brought the donkey and the colt, laid their clothes on them, and set Him on them. ⁸And a very great multitude spread their clothes on the road; others cut down branches from the trees and spread them on the road. ⁹Then the multitudes who went before and those who followed cried out, saying:*

"Hosanna to the Son of David!

'Blessed is He who comes in the name of the LORD!'

Hosanna in the highest!"

[10]And when He had come into Jerusalem, all the city was moved, saying, "Who is this?"

[11]So the multitudes said, "This is Jesus, the prophet from Nazareth of Galilee."

[12]Then Jesus went into the temple of God and drove out all those who bought and sold in the temple, and overturned the tables of the money changers and the seats of those who sold doves. [13]And He said to them, "It is written, 'My house shall be called a house of prayer,' but you have made it a 'den of thieves.'"

[14]Then the blind and the lame came to Him in the temple, and He healed them. [15]But when the chief priests and scribes saw the wonderful things that He did, and the children crying out in the temple and saying, "Hosanna to the Son of David!" they were indignant [16]and said to Him, "Do You hear what these are saying?"

And Jesus said to them, "Yes. Have you never read,

'Out of the mouth of babes and nursing infants

You have perfected praise'?"

[17]Then He left them and went out of the city to Bethany, and He lodged there.

EXPLORATION

1. Do Jesus' instructions at the beginning of this passage strike you as a little odd? Put yourself in the sandals of one of those disciples. What are you feeling and thinking?

2. Isaiah 62:11 and Zechariah 9:9 both prophesy the entrance of Messiah into Jerusalem on a donkey. Why didn't this fact alone convince the masses—for keeps—that Jesus was, in fact, the Christ?

3. Why did Jesus get so angry when he entered the temple area?

4. What were the children doing during this temple-cleansing episode?

5. As all these odd, apparently conflicting events were going on, what were the followers of Jesus doing—those who had spent the previous three years traveling with Jesus, living with him, listening to him, learning from him?

INSPIRATION

Some of us have tried to have a daily quiet time and have not been success-ful. Others of us have a hard time concentrating. And all of us are busy. So rather than spend time with God, listening for his voice, we'll let others spend time with him and then benefit from their experience. Let them tell us what God is saying. After all, isn't that why we pay preachers? Isn't that why we read Christian books? *These folks are good at daily devotions. I'll just learn from them.*

If that is your approach, if your spiritual experiences are secondhand and not firsthand, I'd like to challenge you with this thought: Do you do that with other parts of your life? I don't think so.

You don't do that with vacations. You don't say, "Vacations are such a hassle, packing bags and traveling. I'm going to send someone on vacation for me. When he returns, I'll hear all about it and be spared all the inconvenience." Would you do that? No! You want the experience firsthand . . . Certain things no one can do for you.

You don't do that with romance. You don't say, "I'm in love with that wonderful person, but romance is such a hassle. I'm going to hire a surrogate lover to enjoy the romance in my place. I'll hear all about it and be spared the inconvenience." Who would do that? Perish the thought. You want the romance firsthand . . . Certain things no one can do for you.

You don't let someone eat on your behalf, do you? You don't say, "Chewing is such a bother. My jaws grow so tired, and the variety of tastes is so overwhelming. I'm going to hire someone to chew my food, and I'll just swallow whatever he gives me." Would you do that? Yuck! Of course not! Certain things no one can do for you.

And one of those is spending time with God.

Listening to God is a firsthand experience. When he asks for your attention, God doesn't want you to send a substitute; he wants you. He invites *you* to vacation in his splendor. He invites *you* to feel the touch of his hand. He invites *you* to feast at his table. He wants to spend time with *you*. And with a little training, your time with God can be the highlight of your day. (From *Just Like Jesus* by Max Lucado)

REACTION

6. Do most of your ideas about Christ come from what others have said about him or from your own personal interactions with him?

7. How can a secondhand faith lead to disappointment with Christ?

8. It is one thing to get excited about Jesus in a paradelike, rah-rah atmosphere. It is another matter altogether to be devoted to him and to be one of his daily followers. What factors keep you from a more personal relationship with Jesus?

9. One of the teachings of the New Testament is that Christians are God's temple (1 Cor. 3:16–17; 6:19; 2 Cor. 6:16). Given that fact, what kind of cleansing might Jesus like to do in your own soul?

10. Picture a bunch of kids shouting in the reverent temple courts (v. 15). What does this scenario teach us about worship, about celebration, about excitement over the person of Christ?

11. How can time with the Lord, which leads to deeper intimacy with him, minimize our feelings of disappointment with God?

LIFE LESSONS

Oftentimes God surprises us or disappoints us because our expectations of him do not correspond with his will or with ultimate reality. We may have strong ideas (and wrong ideas) about how life should unfold. But then we crash head-on into God's purposes, and confusion sets in. The solution to this common dilemma is to surrender our opinions and hopes about *what should be* to God's perfect plan (i.e., "what is"). Spend time getting to know the Lord firsthand. When we do this, and when we then approach the situations of life with an open mind and a yielded spirit, we are able to avoid needless disappointment. Remember God isn't whatever we want him to be. He is who he is. And he will do what he will do.

DEVOTION

Lord, so many people were right there. They stood near you and watched you; yet they missed you! They allowed false expectations and the reports of others to keep them from a personal encounter with you. Don't let me make this same mistake. Stir me up so that I will pursue you with passion and come to know you as you truly are.

For more Bible passages on knowing Christ as Messiah, see Matthew 12:22–23; and John 1:44–46; 4:29; 6:42.

To complete the book of Matthew during this twelve-part study, read Matthew 19:1–23:39.

JOURNALING

My biggest disappointments are . . .

LESSON ELEVEN

THE LAST
DAYS

MAX
LUCADO

REFLECTION

Few subjects are as hotly debated among Christians as the subject of the "end times": When will Christ return? What will be the sequence of events? What is Armageddon? What is your current understanding of the last days?

SITUATION

In his final week, Christ gathered his disciples and talked frankly about his second coming. Speaking from the Mount of Olives (where the prophet Zechariah had revealed the Messiah would stand when he comes again to establish his kingdom), Jesus urged his followers to be ready for his return and to be faithful to the end.

OBSERVATION

Read Matthew 24:32–51 from the NCV or the NKJV.

NCV

32"Learn a lesson from the fig tree: When its branches become green and soft and new leaves appear, you know summer is near. 33In the same way, when you see all these things happening, you will know that the time is near, ready to come. 34I tell you the truth, all these things will happen while the people of this time are still living. 35Earth and sky will be destroyed, but the words I have said will never be destroyed.

36"No one knows when that day or time will be, not the angels in heaven, not even the Son. Only the Father knows. 37When the Son of Man comes, it will be like what happened during Noah's time. 38In those days before the flood, people were eating and drinking, marrying and giving their children to be married, until the day Noah entered the boat.

³⁹*They knew nothing about what was happening until the flood came and destroyed them. It will be the same when the Son of Man comes.* ⁴⁰*Two men will be in the field. One will be taken, and the other will be left.* ⁴¹*Two women will be grinding grain with a mill. One will be taken, and the other will be left.*

⁴²*"So always be ready, because you don't know the day your Lord will come.* ⁴³*Remember this: If the owner of the house knew what time of night a thief was coming, the owner would watch and not let the thief break in.* ⁴⁴*So you also must be ready, because the Son of Man will come at a time you don't expect him.*

⁴⁵*"Who is the wise and loyal servant that the master trusts to give the other servants their food at the right time?* ⁴⁶*When the master comes and finds the servant doing his work, the servant will be blessed.* ⁴⁷*I tell you the truth, the master will choose that servant to take care of everything he owns.* ⁴⁸*But suppose that evil servant thinks to himself, 'My master will not come back soon,'* ⁴⁹*and he begins to beat the other servants and eat and get drunk with others like him?* ⁵⁰*The master will come when that servant is not ready and is not expecting him.* ⁵¹*Then the master will cut him in pieces and send him away to be with the hypocrites, where people will cry and grind their teeth with pain."*

NKJV

³²*"Now learn this parable from the fig tree: When its branch has already become tender and puts forth leaves, you know that summer is near.* ³³*So you also, when you see all these things, know that it is near—at the doors!* ³⁴*Assuredly, I say to you, this generation will by no means pass away till all these things take place.* ³⁵*Heaven and earth will pass away, but My words will by no means pass away.*

³⁶*"But of that day and hour no one knows, not even the angels of heaven, but My Father only.* ³⁷*But as the days of Noah were, so also will the coming of the Son of Man be.* ³⁸*For as in the days before the flood, they were eating and drinking, marrying and giving in marriage, until the day that Noah entered the ark,* ³⁹*and did not know until the flood came and took them all away, so also will the coming of the Son of Man be.* ⁴⁰*Then two men will be in the field: one will be taken and the other left.* ⁴¹*Two women will be grinding at the mill: one will be taken and the other left.* ⁴²*Watch therefore, for you do not know what hour your Lord is coming.* ⁴³*But know this, that if the master of the house had known what hour the thief would come, he would have watched and not allowed his house to be broken into.* ⁴⁴*Therefore you also be ready, for the Son of Man is coming at an hour you do not expect.*

⁴⁵*"Who then is a faithful and wise servant, whom his master made ruler over his household, to give them food in due season?* ⁴⁶*Blessed is that servant whom his master, when he comes, will find so doing.* ⁴⁷*Assuredly, I say to you that he will make him ruler over all his goods.* ⁴⁸*But if that evil servant says in his heart, 'My master is delaying his coming,'* ⁴⁹*and begins to beat his fellow servants, and to eat and drink with the drunkards,* ⁵⁰*the master of that servant will come on a day when he is not looking for him and at an hour that he is not aware of,* ⁵¹*and will cut him in two and appoint him his portion with the hypocrites. There shall be weeping and gnashing of teeth."*

EXPLORATION

1. Take a few moments to consider the context of this highlighted passage. How did Christ describe his second coming?

2. What is the lesson from the fig tree?

3. What was Jesus' point in bringing up Noah?

4. When exactly did Jesus say he would come?

5. What is the stern warning of Christ to those who live as though he will never return?

INSPIRATION

As Jesus sought for a way to explain his return, he hearkened back to the flood of Noah. Parallels are obvious. A message of judgment was proclaimed then. It is proclaimed still. People didn't listen then. They refuse to listen today. Noah was sent to save the faithful. Christ was sent to do the same. A flood of water came then. A flood of fire will come next. Noah built a safe place out of wood. Jesus made a safe place with the cross. Those who believed hid in the ark. Those who believe are hidden in Christ.

Most important, what God did in Noah's generation, he will do at Christ's return. He will pronounce a universal, irreversible judgment. A judgment in which grace is revealed, rewards are unveiled, and the impenitent are punished. As you read the story of Noah, you won't find the word *judgment*. But you will find ample evidence of one.

The era of Noah was a sad one. "People on earth did what God said was evil, and violence was everywhere" (Gen. 6:11 NCV). Such rebellion broke the heart of God. "His heart was filled with pain" (Gen. 6:6 NCV). He sent a flood, a mighty purging flood, upon the earth. The skies rained for forty days. "The water rose so much that even the highest mountains under the sky were covered by it. It continued to rise until it was more than twenty feet above the mountains" (Gen. 7:19–20 NCV). Only Noah, his family, and the animals on the ark escaped. Everyone else perished. God didn't slam the gavel on the bench, but he did close the door of the ark. According to Jesus: "It will be the same when the Son of Man comes" (Matt. 24:39 NCV). And so a judgment was rendered.

Talk about a thought that stirs anxiety! Just the term *judgment day* conjures up images of tiny people at the base of a huge bench. On the top of the bench is a book and behind the bench is God and from God comes a voice of judgment—Guilty! *Gulp*. We are supposed to encourage each other with these words? How can the judgment stir anything except panic? For the unprepared, it can't. But for the follower of Jesus who understands the judgment—the hour is not to be dreaded. In fact, once we understand it, we can anticipate it. (From *When Christ Comes* by Max Lucado)

REACTION

6. One of the key elements of the "last days" will be the reality of judgment. Believers will be assessed at the judgment seat of Christ for the purpose of receiving rewards (2 Cor. 5:10). Unbelievers will be judged at the Great White Throne (Rev. 20). What is your honest reaction to this biblical fact?

7. How much effort do you think believers should expend trying to figure out the sequence of end-times events? Why?

8. What signs should we be looking for to know Christ's coming is near?

9. Do you think most believers—do you think *you*—truly live as though Christ could return at any moment? Why or why not?

10. How can we live in preparation for the "at-any-moment" return of Christ? (See 1 Thessalonians 4:13–5:11 and 1 John 2:28 for more.)

11. If all these things are true, name some activities in your life that, in light of eternity, are probably pretty pointless and a waste of time.

LIFE LESSONS

The Old Testament writers predicted the first coming of Christ. And in every case, their prophecies were fulfilled to the letter. Likewise, the New Testament documents contain numerous, explicit details regarding the second coming of Christ. Why should we doubt the veracity of these predictions? The implications for us are clear. If Christ is returning and if his arrival is imminent, how are we living? Do our values and actions square with this ultimate reality? Or are we so focused on this life right now, that we are forgetting the life just ahead? Either we heed and believe the promises of Christ, or we regard them as misguided and/or deceptive. There is no other choice.

DEVOTION

Lord Jesus, while I do not know all the details of your coming, I know the fact of it. You will return to earth. I believe your promises. Therefore, I need to be ready. As I read and reflect upon your word, renew my mind. Give me an eternal perspective that can help me avoid getting caught up in insignificant, worldly affairs.

For more Bible passages on the return of Christ, see Mark 13:1–23; Luke 12:35–40; 1 Corinthians 15:50–57; Titus 2:11–13; and Revelation 19.

To complete the book of Matthew during this twelve-part study, read Matthew 24:1–25:46.

JOURNALING

Some of my unanswered questions about the "end times" are . . .

L E S S O N   T W E L V E

HE'S ALIVE!

MAX LUCADO

REFLECTION

Easter Sunday—the day on which Christians worldwide commemorate the resurrection of Jesus from the dead. Like every other holy day, Easter has become for many a mere holiday, the significance obscured by secular hype. What was Easter like in your home when you were growing up? What traditions or customs did you observe?

SITUATION

An extraordinary life, filled with evolutionary teachings and jaw-dropping miracles, and ending with a horrific death. Only that wasn't the end. Matthew, like all the Gospel writers, concludes his account of the Carpenter-turned-King by demonstrating the authority of Jesus Christ over death itself. Matthew ends with a Messiah who is very much alive . . . and eager for the whole world to know it.

OBSERVATION

Read Matthew 28:1–10 from the NCV or the NKJV.

NCV

¹*The day after the Sabbath day was the first day of the week. At dawn on the first day, Mary Magdalene and another woman named Mary went to look at the tomb.*

²*At that time there was a strong earthquake. An angel of the Lord came down from heaven, went to the tomb, and rolled the stone away from the entrance. Then he sat on the stone.* ³*He was shining as bright as lightning, and his clothes were white as snow.* ⁴*The soldiers guarding the tomb shook with fear because of the angel, and they became like dead men.* ⁵*The angel said to the women, "Don't be afraid. I know that you are looking for Jesus, who has been crucified.* ⁶*He is not here. He has risen from the dead as he said he would. Come and see the place where his body was.* ⁷*And go quickly and tell his followers, 'Jesus has risen from the dead. He is going into Galilee ahead of you, and you will see him there.'" Then the angel said, "Now I have told you."*

8The women left the tomb quickly. They were afraid, but they were also very happy. They ran to tell Jesus' followers what had happened. 9Suddenly, Jesus met them and said, "Greetings." The women came up to him, took hold of his feet, and worshiped him. 10Then Jesus said to them, "Don't be afraid. Go and tell my followers to go on to Galilee, and they will see me there."

NKJV

1Now after the Sabbath, as the first day of the week began to dawn, Mary Magdalene and the other Mary came to see the tomb. 2And behold, there was a great earthquake; for an angel of the Lord descended from heaven, and came and rolled back the stone from the door, and sat on it. 3His countenance was like lightning, and his clothing as white as snow. 4And the guards shook for fear of him, and became like dead men.

5But the angel answered and said to the women, "Do not be afraid, for I know that you seek Jesus who was crucified. 6He is not here; for He is risen, as He said. Come, see the place where the Lord lay. 7And go quickly and tell His disciples that He is risen from the dead, and indeed He is going before you into Galilee; there you will see Him. Behold, I have told you."

8So they went out quickly from the tomb with fear and great joy, and ran to bring His disciples word.

9And as they went to tell His disciples, behold, Jesus met them, saying, "Rejoice!" So they came and held Him by the feet and worshiped Him. 10Then Jesus said to them, "Do not be afraid. Go and tell My brethren to go to Galilee, and there they will see Me."

EXPLORATION

1. On what day did the women visit Christ's tomb?

2. What specific supernatural events does Matthew claim took place on that first Easter morning?

3. Whom did the women meet and what did he say?

4. How does Matthew describe the mood of the women?

5. What transpired as the women left to find the other followers of Jesus?

INSPIRATION

The empty tomb never resists honest investigation. A lobotomy is not a pre-requisite of discipleship. Following Christ demands faith, but not blind faith. "Come and see," the angel invites. Shall we?

Take a look at the vacated tomb. Did you know the opponents of Christ never challenged its vacancy? No Pharisee or Roman soldier ever led a contingent back to the burial site and declared, "The angel was wrong. The body is here. It was all a rumor."

They would have if they could have. Within weeks disciples occupied every Jerusalem street corner, announcing a risen Christ. What quicker way for the enemies of the church to shut them up than to produce a cold and lifeless body? Display the cadaver, and Christianity is stillborn. But they had no cadaver to display.

Helps explain the Jerusalem revival. When the apostles argued for the empty tomb, the people looked to the Pharisees for a rebuttal. But they had none to give. As A. M. Fairbairn put it long ago, "The silence of the Jews is as eloquent as the speech of the Christians!"

Speaking of the Christians, remember the followers' fear at the crucifixion? They ran. Scared as cats in a dog pound. Peter cursed Christ at the fire. Emmaus-bound disciples bemoaned the death of Christ on the trail. After the crucifixion, *"the disciples were meeting behind locked doors because they were afraid of the Jewish leaders"* (John 20:19 NLT).

These guys were so chicken we could call the Upper Room a henhouse.

But fast-forward forty days. Bankrupt traitors have become a force of life-changing fury. Peter is preaching in the very precinct where Christ was arrested. Followers of Christ defy the enemies of Christ. Whip them and they'll worship. Lock them up and they'll launch a jailhouse ministry. As bold after the Resurrection as they were cowardly before it.

Explanation:

Greed? They made no money.

Power? They gave all the credit to Christ.

Popularity? Most were killed for their beliefs.

Only one explanation remains—a resurrected Christ and his Holy Spirit. The courage of these men and women was forged in the fire of the empty tomb. The disciples did not dream up a resurrection. The Resurrection fired up the disciples. Have doubts about the empty tomb? Come and see the disciples. (From *Next Door Savior* by Max Lucado)

REACTION

6. Do you agree with this conclusion—that there is no other compelling explanation for the radical change among the disciples except that they must have seen the resurrected Christ?

7. In the first century, Jewish women would not have been regarded as credible witnesses. How does this fact lend authenticity to the gospel claim that two women were the first to see Christ alive?

8. Matthew 28:11–15 tells of a plan concocted by the Jewish leaders and the Roman guards to deny the story of a resurrected Christ. Why is this story so obviously false?

9. Matthew 28:17 suggests that some (and "some" would seem to mean at least three) of Jesus' followers struggled with doubt—even though he was right there! Do you ever find it hard to trust in Christ?

10. If Christ was able to raise others from the dead, and if he himself conquered death, what are the implications for us?

11. Look ahead to the very end of Matthew 28. What were Jesus' final words to his followers?

LIFE LESSONS

Matthew's Gospel, from start to finish, is filled with gloriously good news. Immanuel . . . God with us. The sinless one, impervious to Satan's temptations. The messiah-king who offers citizenship in the now and not-yet kingdom of God. The compassionate healer. The ingenious teacher. The almighty miracle-worker. The Lord of the Sabbath. The enemy of false religion. The Son of David. The crucified Savior. The resurrected Lord who possesses all authority in heaven and on earth. The returning Son of Man. Christ is all these things and more. This is our message. *He* is our message!

DEVOTION

Father, thank you for sending your Son. What an incredible gift, and what an extraordinary life! By his death and resurrection Jesus is more than able to save me from the penalty and power of sin. Now, may the Spirit of the living Christ reign in me, giving me the power to live as you command.

For more Bible passages on Christ's (and our) victory over death, see Psalm 23:4; Hosea 13:14; Romans 8:2; 1 Corinthians 15:54–57; and Ephesians 2:4–5.

To complete the book of Matthew during this twelve-part study, read Matthew 26:1–28:20.